W9-CYF-946

WHEN IN
ROME

The Ultimate Study-Abroad Guide

Writer: Kim Westerman

SparkNotes would like to thank Margo Orlando for her editorial contribution to this book.

See page 219 for a list of photo credits.

© 2008 by Spark Publishing

All rights reserved. No part of this publication may be reproduced, stored in a retrieval system, or transmitted, in any form or by any means, electronic, mechanical, photocopying, recording, or otherwise, without prior written permission from the publisher.

SPARKNOTES is a registered trademark of SparkNotes LLC.

Spark Publishing
A Division of Barnes & Noble
120 Fifth Avenue
New York, NY 10011
www.sparknotes.com

Library of Congress Cataloging-in-Publication Data

When in Rome: live like a local.

p. cm.—(When in—)

ISBN-13: 978-1-4114-9847-1 (pbk.)
ISBN-10: 1-4114-9847-X (pbk.)

1. Rome (Italy)—Description and travel. 2. Rome (Italy)—Guidebooks. I. Spark Publishing.

DG806.2.W44 2007
914.5'6320493—dc22

                                                      2007029547

Please submit changes or report errors to www.sparknotes.com/errors.

Printed and bound in the United States

10 9 8 7 6 5 4 3 2 1

Although every effort has been made to ensure that this book is accurate at press time, be advised that given the nature of the information set forth in this book, the prices, addresses, telephone numbers, and other travel details listed herein are subject to change. Accordingly, the author and publisher make no warranty about the accuracy or completeness of the book's content. The author and publisher disclaim all liability to any party for any loss, damage, injury, disruption to travel plans, or other loss or inconvenience resulting from the use of this book.

A NOTE FROM SPARKNOTES

Congratulations on your decision to study abroad! Living in a new country, whether for a semester, a year, or longer, will enlighten you in ways you can't even imagine. Today, many consider travel abroad to be an essential step in a young person's education. Immersing yourself in a new culture, among new people, places, and things, will not only broaden your worldview, but also better equip you to face the challenges of a rapidly globalizing future.

We created the *When In* series to help you make the most of your time abroad. This book is intended for those who have already been accepted into a study-abroad program or have made the decision to live overseas. Your college or university will advise you about choosing a program, prerequisites and academic requirements, paperwork, and financial arrangements, so our focus is on the next step: the challenges you'll face as you settle into your new life. Our goal is to give you *exactly* what you need to know to make a smooth transition and get the most out of your time abroad.

Unlike traditional travel guides, the *When In* series focuses on the basics of living daily life as a study-abroad student:

- Nuts-and-bolts information, from finding housing to setting up a bank account to getting medical care

- The inside scoop on living on a student's budget

- The city's coolest restaurants, bars, clubs, study spots, and other places to hang out with friends

- Concise information on art, theater, film, music, sporting events, and other activities to keep you busy and involved in city life

With your *When In* guide, you'll *live like a local* in no time. Good luck!

Got comments? Your feedback makes us better. Contact us at www.sparknotes.com/comments.

KEY TO SYMBOLS

We use the following symbols throughout this guide:

Ⓐ	Address
Ⓣ	Telephone number
Ⓦ	Website
Ⓜ	Metro stop

10 TIPS FOR MAKING THE MOST OF YOUR TIME ABROAD

1. *Do* make friends with the locals. This will be one of the most rewarding aspects of your stay. Now's not the time to hold back!

2. *Do* take seriously every opportunity to practice speaking a new language. Immersing yourself in the language day in and day out will speed your learning process.

3. *Don't* worry about what you're missing back home. Do your best to live in the moment and embrace this amazing opportunity.

4. *Do* take advantage of cheap flights and train fares. You'll likely have frequent breaks—or, at least, greater freedom than you're used to—and it's easy and affordable to take weekend or even weeklong trips to new places.

5. *Do* keep a journal, create a blog, snap pictures, shoot videos, or otherwise record your time abroad. You'll want to remember and share all the details.

6. *Don't* be afraid to speak up if you find yourself facing anti-Americanism or stereotypes. Remember that you can counter negative stereotypes by setting a good example abroad.

7. *Don't* let culture shock get you down. Confusion is a normal part of travel, and only by taking time to settle in and make friends will you conquer it.

8. *Do* immerse yourself in the local culture. Eat what the locals eat. Shop where they shop. If you can't find a familiar item from home, live without it.

9. *Don't* embark on your experience with assumptions or preconceptions. Your new life will surprise you in every possible way—and you should let it.

10. *Don't* view your study-abroad time as your one and only chance to experience life abroad. Relish the everyday moments and reassure yourself that you'll be back!

Other titles in the *When In* series include:

When In London
When In Madrid
When In Paris

CONTENTS

INTRODUCTION 1
  History 1
  Culture 3
  University Life 3
  Living on the Cheap 4
  10 Books and 10 Films to Check Out Before You Leave 7

1. PAPERWORK & PRACTICALITIES 9
  Passports 10
  Student Visas 11
  Study-Abroad Checklist 15
  10 Songs to Download for Your Flight to Rome 17

2. THE NEIGHBORHOODS 19
  Colosseum/Esquiline 20
  Jewish Ghetto/Campo de' Fiori 21
  Nomentano 22
  Piazza Navona/Pantheon 23
  The Spanish Steps/Via Vittorio Veneto/Parioli 24
  Stazione Termini/San Lorenzo 25
  Testaccio 25
  Trastevere 26
  Vatican City 27
  5 Places Where You'll Find American Students 29

3. GETTING AROUND 31
  Metro 32
  Buses and Trams 35
  Taxis 37
  Bikes 38
  Cars and Scooters 39
  Trains 40
  To and From the Airports 41
  5 Things That Will Make You Think,
  "Now That's Rome" 43

4. FINDING HOUSING 45
  Apartment Listings 46
  Brokers 48
  Apartment Prices 49
  Leases 50

Homestays 51
5 Roman Apartment Quirks 53

5. SHOPPING 55
Supermarkets 56
Specialty Foods 58
Farmers' Markets 60
Flea Markets 62
One-Stop Shopping 63
Home Furnishings 63
High-Traffic Shopping Areas 64
5 Great Gifts to Send Home 65

6. DAILY LIVING 67
Getting Money 68
Italian Bank Accounts 71
Postal Services 72
Apartment Living 73
5 Affordable City Adventures 77

7. STUDYING & STAYING INFORMED 79
Places to Study 80
Libraries 81
English-Language Bookstores 82
Newspapers 83
Magazines 84
TV and Radio 85
5 Good Excuses Not to Study 87

8. STAYING IN TOUCH 89
Internet 90
Cell Phones 91
Calling Home 92
*5 Things About the United States You Won't Expect
to Miss—but Will* 95

9. HEALTH 97
Health Insurance 98
Pharmacies 101
Visiting the Doctor 103
Sexual Health Issues 105
5 Ideas for Conquering Homesickness 107

10. GETTING INVOLVED 109
Meeting Locals 110
Clubs, Organizations, and Other Resources 113
5 Free Ways to Impress Your Date 117

11. WORKING 119
Job Hunting 120
Types of Jobs 121
Getting Paperwork in Order 124
5 Small Luxuries to Request from Home 125

12. FITNESS & BEAUTY 127
Gyms and Sports Clubs 128
Swimming Pools 129
Running Routes 130
Yoga and Pilates 130
Hair Salons and Barbershops 131
Spas 132
5 Cheap, Touristy Things You've Got to Do 133

13. SPORTS 135
Recreational Sports 136
Spectator Sports 139
*5 More Reasons to Love Rome (As If You Needed
More Reasons . . .)* 141

14. CULTURAL ACTIVITIES 143
Museums and Galleries 144
Guided Sightseeing Tours 146
Performing Arts 147
Films 150
Festivals and Holidays 152
5 Affordable Day Trips 155

15. EATING OUT 157
Dinner with Friends 158
Dinner with Family 160
Date Spots 162
Vegetarian 163
Late Night Food 164
Lunch/Food to Go 165
5 Almost Free Ways to Spend an Evening with Friends ... 167

16. NIGHT LIFE 169
Bars 170
Clubs 172
Live Music 173
Gay/Lesbian Bars and Clubs 175
Other Activities 175
*5 Cool Drinks You Won't Find at Your College Bar
Back Home* 177

17. GOING AWAY 179
Eurail 180
Trenitalia 181
Air Travel 183
Package Trips and Tours 184
Renting a Car 186
*5 Affordable Ways to Spend Your Spring or
Midterm Break* 189

18. EMERGENCIES 191
Important Phone Numbers 192
Getting Cited or Arrested 195
Lost or Stolen Property 196
Replacing a Passport 197
Unexpected Trips Home 198

APPENDIX 201
Useful Phrases 202
Conversions 215
Clothing Sizes 216
Country Codes 217

ABOUT THE WRITER 218

INDEX 221

INTRODUCTION

The Colosseum. The Roman Forum. The Pantheon. Vespas taking turns at breakneck speed. Heaping plates of pasta. Long, long lunches. Copious amounts of wine and espresso. Your ideas of Rome will probably encompass these images and more. Of all the cities in the world, few capture the imagination as intensely as Rome does.

The truth is that Rome is home to millions of people whose concerns about life, school, and work will probably seem pretty familiar. But as you settle in, keep your eyes and mind open to the many ways that past meets present. Notice, for instance, how tiny, ultra-modern Smart cars are parked in front of oversized medieval structures—or how chic clothing boutiques sit just steps away from seventeenth-century fountains fed by fourth-century (B.C.E.!) aqueducts. You're sure to be continually charmed and enlightened by the surprises that await you.

HISTORY

According to legend, Rome was founded by twin brothers Romulus and Remus, descendents of Mars, the god of war. Mythology aside, there is truth to the old saying: Rome wasn't built in a day. Tremendous amounts of military and political prowess were required to turn a small pastoral settlement into the cradle of one of the world's greatest civilizations. Such are the origins of the republic founded in the fifth century B.C.E. and the empire whose power spread across what is modern-day Europe from the first century B.C.E. until its fall in the fifth century C.E.

A slow and steady decline from greatness culminated when the Visigoths sacked Rome in 410 B.C.E., an invasion that ultimately led to the fall of the entire Western Roman

Empire in 476. The Middle Ages found Rome a diseased and desolate place, and only in the fifteenth century did Rome begin to regain any glory. After the Catholic Church's Great Schism, Pope Martin V used church funds to refurbish Rome during his reign from 1417 to 1431. For the next few centuries, wealthy papal families commissioned the many Renaissance and Baroque structures that make the city so breathtaking today. Many of Rome's most beloved structures, including the Spanish Steps, were constructed during this period.

In the eighteenth and nineteenth centuries, control of Rome changed hands a number of times. In 1870, troops led by the Piedmontese King Vittorio Emanuele II breached the city walls near the Porta Pia and conquered Rome, unifying Italy as a nation. Rome became its capital, and the Vatican a separate state.

From the time of unification through World War II, Rome's topography changed drastically. New government buildings, streets, residential neighborhoods, and train stations were built. Under Benito Mussolini's fascist government (1922–1943), ancient ruins were unearthed as part of the regime's ideological identification with the ancient empire. Neighborhoods were leveled to make way for broader avenues that created better views and traffic flow, and entire new business and residential zones were constructed. Much of today's iconic Rome—the area around the Colosseum, the Esposizione Universale di Roma area, and the Via della Conciliazione leading to St Peter's Square—was designed in the 1930s. Despite occupation by the Nazis, Rome's landscape emerged from World War II relatively unscathed.

The city keeps growing, and today it battles typical urban problems such as traffic flow. Currently under careful construction are two new metro lines that will wind through as-yet-unearthed ancient ruins in the city center, providing modern convenience without disrupting ancient foundations. The metro project in many ways emblematizes Rome's contradictory nature and its largest challenge: to be a livable, modern city while allowing the ancient past to live and breathe.

CULTURE

Roman life is a fascinating combination of chaos and peace. You'll rarely sit for breakfast, but instead will grab a quick coffee and *cornetto* (a roll filled with custard or jam) on your way to class. At dinner, you're likely to have a hurry-up-and-wait experience, racing across town to beat the crowds to your favorite haunt so that you can sit for hours, getting your bill only when you're ready for it (and often long after you ask for it). In Rome, there's a lot to do, but fitting it all in can be difficult—especially if you're on a schedule *and* a budget. Shopping is expensive, store and museum hours are variable and often short, and there's just no end to the possibilities of exhibitions, movies, concerts, or plays you can attend.

Although Rome is a modern, cosmopolitan city, the cozy, villagelike feel of Italian life is strong here. The family is of primary importance, and Italian culture emphasizes strong ties across many generations. Because of this emphasis, along with economic necessity, older family members sometimes live with their adult children. It's not unusual, either, for young people to live with their parents until they reach their thirties. Romans place a great deal of pride in their country's many traditions, from family to food to football.

UNIVERSITY LIFE

Although Italians will tell you that their university system is becoming increasingly Americanized every year, two major differences define the student experience in Italy. First, a university education costs practically nothing, and second, the system is composed almost entirely of public universities. The numerous young Italians who can therefore take advantage of the system have a choice between a *laurea breve* (three-year) degree program, which often leads right to employment, or a more intensive *laurea normale* (five-year) program, which generally indicates interest in pursuing further studies.

The academic year appears similar to that of American universities, but the scheduling details are very different. Fall courses often begin in early October, and exams are held after the holidays through the month of January. Spring semester begins later and normally finishes in July, although breaks and exam schedules vary by class or year of study. Students do not take exams for spring classes until the week before classes start again in October. Because exams are often based on broad, independent reading that must be studied in addition to the material discussed in the classroom, students frequently choose to spend their time studying independently rather than going to class.

Rome offers many study-abroad programs and universities, but these are scattered around the city, and Rome is simply too big to have a college-town feel. In addition, Italian universities are structured more like American commuter campuses than residential ones, so don't expect dorms or student unions to function as default meeting places.

LIVING ON THE CHEAP

Like most of the world's greatest cities, Rome is expensive—and the terrible exchange rate will add to the strain on your wallet. Stretching your euros is by no means an insurmountable challenge, however. Here are some basics to get you started:

- **Student ID:** As a student, you'll have access to numerous discounts all over the city. Always show your ID and ask for a discount at movie theaters, bookstores, and (especially) galleries and museums, even if one isn't advertised: Lenient clerks may just have some sympathy for you. Be sure, also, to ask about student discounts whenever you buy tickets for shows or book any travel.

- **International Student ID and Exchange Cards:** An International Student Identity Card (ISIC) or International Student Exchange Card (ISE Card) will give you discounts on hostels, restaurants, tours, clubs, and attractions in more than 100 countries, as well as access to emergency helplines, health insurance, and other benefits. Some cards also offer discounts on international phone calls, airfares, and shopping. See www.isecard.com or www.istc.org for details.

- **Food shopping:** Of course you'll want to get out and explore Rome, but it's also very Roman to spend a night at home with friends. Cook up some simple pasta—spending €0.60 for a whole box instead of €10 for one plate—and get a bottle of cheap wine at any neighborhood wine shop, where €8 or less will buy your choice from an amazing local selection. For buying fruits and vegetables, you'll be surprised at how economical Rome's many open-air markets can be (for more information and specific locations, see "Farmers' Markets" in Chapter 5).

- **Eating out:** When you do go out to eat, choose wisely. Avoid restaurants right on the touristy squares: They always charge more, and the food may be lower quality. Head to the back streets instead.

- **Movies:** All theaters offer discounted prices on Wednesday nights. Why not make a ritual of seeing a mid-week movie?

- **Free events:** Scour the weekly pamphlet *Roma C'è,* available at any newsstand, to find out what free events are offered in the city. You'll be surprised at how many there are. You can find the online version at www.romace.it.

- **Transportation:** You'll rarely have a reason to take a taxi in such a walkable and well-connected city. If you take public transportation, consider purchasing monthly or annual bus/metro passes, which are reasonably priced for students and more convenient than single-trip tickets.

10 BOOKS AND 10 FILMS TO CHECK OUT BEFORE YOU LEAVE

When you make the move to Rome, what exactly will you be in for? Only time will tell. But to get a first glimpse of the Eternal City *and* to get in the mood for Rome, try these books and films:

BOOKS

1. *Angels and Demons*, Dan Brown
2. *The Smiles of Rome*, Susan Cahill
3. *The Food of Love*, Anthony Capella
4. *The Accusers*, Lindsey Davis
5. *Rome: The Biography of a City*, Christopher Hibbert
6. *Eat, Pray, Love*, Elizabeth Gilbert
7. *Cabaret: A Roman Riddle*, Lily Prior
8. *Household Gods*, Judith Tarr and Harry Turtledove
9. *When in Rome*, Gemma Townley
10. *The Italians*, Luigi Barzini

FILMS

1. *The Bicycle Thief* (1948), Vittorio de Sica
2. *Roman Holiday* (1953), William Wyler
3. *Ben-Hur* (1959), William Wyler
4. *La Dolce Vita* (1960), Federico Fellini
5. *Spartacus* (1960), Stanley Kubrick
6. *Yesterday, Today, and Tomorrow* (1963), Vittorio de Sica
7. *History of the World: Part 1* (1981), Mel Brooks
8. *Life is Beautiful* (1997), Roberto Benigni
9. *The Talented Mr. Ripley* (1999), Anthony Minghella
10. *Gladiator* (2000), Ridley Scott

1. Paperwork & Practicalities

Rome's delights are unparalleled, and spontaneous exploration will reward you infinitely—but you'll need to plan certain details ahead of time. The first order of business is getting a passport. If you already have one, make sure it won't expire while you're away. You'll also need to get a student visa. Be sure to apply well before you'll need both documents, as they can take six weeks or more to process.

Your college or university will likely guide you through your passport and visa applications, but in this chapter we'll give you a crash course so you know exactly what to expect. Once you've taken care of the nuts and bolts, you can get to the fun parts of life abroad—like figuring out the fastest way to get from Fiumicino airport to a heaping plate of pasta.

PASSPORTS

If you've never held a U.S. passport, you can apply for one in person at your local passport facility (there are more than 8,000 such facilities in the United States). If you're renewing your passport, apply by mail *unless* your most current passport has been damaged, lost, or stolen, or was issued when you were under sixteen. Standard processing time for passports is six weeks; expedited service, with an extra fee, takes two weeks. Most passports are valid for ten years. You can find all the information you need about applying for a passport, including the location of the nearest passport facility, at www.travel.state.gov.

PASSPORT CHECKLIST

Here's what you need to bring with you when you apply for a passport:

✔ Fee payment, which is currently $97

- ✔ A completed application form (available online)

- ✔ Two identical passport-size photos

- ✔ A birth certificate or other proof of U.S. citizenship

- ✔ A valid photo ID

LOSE YOUR PASSPORT?

If you lose your passport during your time in Rome, head directly to the passport office at the U.S. Embassy—no appointment is necessary. If your passport expires while you're abroad, you can also renew it through the U.S. Embassy. For more information on dealing with a lost or stolen passport, see "Replacing a Passport" in Chapter 18.

U.S. Embassy in Rome Ⓐ Via Vittorio Veneto 121, Ⓣ 06 4674 2244, Ⓦ www.rome.usembassy. gov, Ⓜ Spagna or Barberini

STUDENT VISAS

You need to apply for a visa in person at an Italian consulate, which, depending on where you live, could be quite a haul to get to. To ensure that you don't make a long trip in vain, *be as thorough as possible* in putting together your application beforehand. Also check your regional consulate's website for information on what documents you'll need to bring with you, as requirements may vary. Applications can take up to six weeks to process. You can find the location of the consulate in your region on the website of Italy's Ministry of Foreign Affairs, www.esteri.it/visti/index_eng.asp.

STUDENT VISA CHECKLIST

Here's what you'll probably need to bring with you when you apply for a student visa. Be sure to check this against your regional consulate's website, as requirements vary:

- ✔ One filled-out copy of the downloadable application form

- ✔ Your passport, which must be valid for at least four months beyond the period requested for the visa, along with a photocopy of the page bearing your name and birth date

- ✔ One recent passport-size photo

- ✔ Your current student ID and a photocopy of it

- ✔ Information on your study abroad program (including a copy of your acceptance letter)

- ✔ Proof that you'll have economic support of at least $1,000 per month while in Italy (such as a bank statement or a letter from your university stating that tuition has been paid)

- ✔ Proof of health insurance

In addition to obtaining a visa, any U.S. citizen who plans to live in Italy for longer than three months must obtain a *permesso di soggiorno* (visitor's permit) from a *questura* (state police office) in Rome. Be sure to bring your passport and visa when you go to request this permit. Within two months, you will be mailed a certificate of residence. Here's where to go.

Rome questura Ⓐ Via San Vitale 15, Ⓣ 06 46861, Ⓜ Repubblica

REGISTERING WITH THE U.S. EMBASSY

It's always a good idea to register your trip with the U.S. Embassy in Rome at https://travelregistration.state.gov/ibrs/ (choose the "long-term traveler" option if you'll be abroad for longer than six months). By providing information about your stay and your emergency contacts, you'll help the embassy find you quickly in the case of an emergency back home (or abroad). The embassy can also offer assistance if you're involved in an accident or a crime—see Chapter 18, "Emergencies," for more information on what to do in these situations.

OTHER TYPES OF VISAS

If you hope to extend your stay after classes end or if you have a nonstudent significant other who will be joining you during your time abroad, you should know about three other types of visas:

- **Work visa:** A work visa is required for any nonstudent who intends to work in Italy. Work visas are notoriously difficult to get and require applicants to first find Italian employers willing to sponsor them. For more information on work visas, see Chapter 11, "Working."

- **Family visa:** If you are legally married and already residing in Italy with a valid work or student visa, your spouse may join you on a family visa. You must provide a copy of your marriage certificate, as well as proof that your spouse is a U.S. citizen (or has a green card). You must also obtain a *nulla osta*—a letter from the Rome *questura* granting your spouse permission to accompany you. If you and your partner are not legally married, you will need to apply for a *visa elletiva* (an extended-stay, nonimmigrant visa). You will essentially need to meet the same requirements as your partner did to obtain a student or work visa. However, be aware that Italian authorities are much more rigorous about looking into your proof of financial support if you are not a registered student.

- **Tourist visa:** Tourists who are just visiting Rome don't need to worry about visas. The stamp you get in your passport is considered a "tourist visa," and it permits you to visit countries in the Schengen area, an open-border zone whose participating countries include Austria, Belgium, Denmark, Finland, France, Germany, Greece, Iceland, Italy, Luxembourg, the Netherlands, Norway, Portugal, and Sweden. You're free to visit for up to ninety days over a six-month period, which begins on the day your passport is stamped when you enter Europe. The ninety days do not have to be consecutive, and days spent outside the Schengen area—for example, for a trip to London or Krakow—don't count against the total. After ninety days, the tourist visa expires and can be renewed only after the six-month period is up.

KEEPING IT LEGAL

If you enter Italy on a tourist visa and stay longer than ninety days over a six-month period, guess what? You're an illegal alien. When you attempt to leave or reenter Italy, or should you have a run-in with police, you may be detained, deported, or forced to pay hefty fines.

STUDY-ABROAD CHECKLIST

Before packing your bags and heading to the airport with a big ole' excited grin on your face, make sure you've checked the following off your list:

✔ Get a **passport.**

✔ Get a **student visa.**

✔ Book your **plane ticket.**

✔ Arrange **housing** if it's not already provided for you, or find a hotel/hostel if you plan to conduct an apartment search once you've arrived in Rome (see Chapter 4, "Finding Housing").

✔ Apply for an International Student Identity Card (**ISIC**), which can get you great discounts on travel, entertainment, and more (see "Living on the Cheap" in the Introduction).

✔ Set up **online financial statements** and automatic bill payment.

✔ Arrange for **absentee voting** if you'll be abroad during an election.

✔ Schedule a predeparture **physical** if you need one. You don't need to get any particular vaccinations before going to Italy as long as your routine vaccinations, such as tetanus-diphtheria and measles, are up to date.

✔ Get a copy of your **medical records,** especially if you have a preexisting condition for which you'll need treatment abroad.

✔ Make sure you have adequate **health insurance** coverage (your university should help with this). See Chapter 9, "Health," for more information about insurance options and getting medical treatment while in Rome.

✔ Set up **VoIP service** with your friends and family so you can keep in touch for free (see Chapter 8, "Staying in Touch").

✔ Refill any **prescription drugs** you need (see Chapter 9, "Health," for your options when it comes to buying prescription medications in Rome).

✔ Stock up on **over-the-counter drugs** such as aspirin and cold medicine. Your American drugs will come in handy down the line when you need to restock your medicine cabinet—showing the Roman pharmacist your American product may help him or her find you the Roman equivalent.

✔ Make a **photocopy of your passport** and leave it, along with your contact info in Rome, with your family.

✔ Call your **credit card** companies to inform them that you'll be abroad so you don't receive concerned phone calls that someone is using your card overseas.

✔ Stock up on **American products** you may not be able to get abroad, such as your favorite brands of deodorant, hair products, or moisturizer.

✔ Stock up on **clothes** and other essentials (you'll find prices to be much higher than in the United States—especially since you'll be paying in euros and sales happen just twice a year).

✔ Consider **traveling light.** If you're studying abroad in the spring, you won't need many sweaters. And though you may love your dress shoes, you may feel differently about them after navigating cobblestones in high heels.

✔ Enough already. Now **get going!**

10 SONGS TO DOWNLOAD FOR YOUR FLIGHT TO ROME

1. "Mambo Italiano," Rosemary Clooney
2. "Arrivederci Roma," Nat King Cole
3. "Rome Wasn't Built in a Day," Sam Cooke
4. "Seven Nights in Rome," the Rippingtons and Russ Freeman
5. "Al di là," Al Hirt
6. "When in Rome," Billy Joel
7. "On an Evening in Roma," Dean Martin
8. "All Roads Lead to Rome," the Stranglers
9. "The Spanish Steps of Rome," Toto
10. "Grazie Roma," Antonello Venditti

2. The Neighborhoods

Rome was built on and around seven hills. To this day, these famous hills provide the demarcation lines between the city's diverse neighborhoods—along with excellent bird's-eye views of your new home. The classic tourist attractions are centered in the Colosseum, Piazza Navona/Pantheon, and Vatican City areas, while real Roman life throbs in the Spanish Steps/Via Vittorio Veneto neighborhood, the Stazione Termini/San Lorenzo area, and the Testaccio and Jewish Ghetto/Campo de' Fiori areas.

There is one common denominator among all of Rome's neighborhoods: the intersection of the ancient with the modern. You might be at a chic outdoor cafe near the Spanish Steps and discover a woman hanging out her laundry next to a fourteenth-century relief on the roof above your head. Or perhaps you'll immerse yourself in a Caravaggio painting at a quiet, dimly lit church only to walk outside and head directly for a hip coffee bar. These are the kinds of fascinating juxtapositions you'll encounter on a daily basis.

COLOSSEUM/ESQUILINE
Metro: Cavour, Colosseo, Vittorio Emanuele

The heart of ancient Rome, the Colosseum is clogged with tourists during high season (summertime as well as Easter, Christmas, and New Year's Eve). It's a must-see for every visitor—both for the gladiator amphitheater itself as well as for the sites that branch off from it, most notably the Roman Forum and Basilica di Santa Maria Maggiore (arguably the second-most famous church in the city, after St Peter's). In Esquiline, you'll find more non-Italians than anywhere else in Rome, making the neighborhood one of Rome's most multi-ethnic destinations.

WHAT YOU'LL SEE:

- The **Colosseum** and, just outside it, men dressed in full gladiator costumes posing for pictures amid the throngs of tourists. Ⓜ Colosseo
- **Villa Celimontana,** a Renaissance villa with gorgeous city views. Ⓜ Colosseo
- **Basilica di San Clemente,** a twelfth-century church that sits on layers of earlier buildings close to Colosseum. Ⓐ Via di San Giovanni in Laterano, Ⓣ 06 7045 1018, Ⓜ Colosseo
- More ancient glories than you can imagine, including the **Roman Forum** (Ⓜ Colosseo), **Palatine Hill** (Ⓜ Colosseo), and **Capitoline Museums** (Bus Piazza Venezia).
- **Via Panisperna,** where Enrico Fermi and other young physicists carried out their infamous experiments on nuclear radioactivity in 1934. Ⓜ Cavour

JEWISH GHETTO/CAMPO DE' FIORI
Bus: **Campo de' Fiori**

These adjacent neighborhoods are similar in character: Both are laid-back places where Romans live. The houses and apartments have that sun-bleached ochre hue that Italian restaurants in the United States try to emulate—but here it's the real deal. In the Jewish Ghetto, you'll find kosher restaurants and butchers. And in *il Campo* (the Campo de' Fiori) you'll find Rome's most famous outdoor market: the best place in the city to buy local (and often organic) fruits, vegetables, meats, and cheeses.

WHAT YOU'LL SEE:

- Hordes of Italian and international students drinking beer and wine—and occasionally getting into late-night scuffles—at **il Campo's bars.**
- Buildings on the **Via del Biscione,** just off the northeast end of il Campo, whose exteriors are curved because they are built over the ruins of the ancient semicircular **Theater of Pompeii** (55 B.C.E.). Bus Campo de' Fiori

- The **Tiber Island,** an island with a 2,800-year-old hospital.
- €20 jeans and other good bargains in the discount shops on the **Via dei Giubbonari.** Bus Campo de' Fiori
- The charming sixteenth-century **Turtle fountain,** in the Ghetto's Piazza Mattei. Bus/Tram Largo di Torre Argentina
- The ancient **Teatro di Marcello.** Ⓐ Via del Teatro di Marcello 44
- The ruins of **Portico d'Ottavia.** Ⓐ Via Portico d'Ottavia, Bus Via del Teatro di Marcello
- The **Largo 16 Ottobre,** a square (near the stunning synagogue) commemorating the deportation of Roman Jews to Nazi concentration camps. Bus Via del Teatro di Marcello

NOMENTANO
Bus: Via Nomentana

Characterized by the Villa Torlonia at its center, Nomentano offers great bargains on rent for those who want to live in the northern part of the city—and it's strangely fascinating to jog or walk the grounds where Mussolini lived with his wife and children. The villa itself is still there, but it's fallen into disrepair. Nomentano also has amazing family-owned markets, hardware stores, and clothing shops, giving the neighborhood a homey feel.

WHAT YOU'LL SEE:

- **Villa Paganini,** a park, complete with a charming garden and children playing. Bus Via Nomentana
- **Dei Gracchi,** one of Rome's best *gelaterie* (ice cream parlors). Ⓐ Viale Regina Margherita 212, Ⓣ 06 321 6668, Bus Regina Margherita
- **Porta Pia,** a gate designed by Michelangelo—and the approximate site of the Imperial army's entry into the city in 1870 (ultimately uniting Italy). Bus Via XX Settembre

- **Via del Corso,** a crowded shopping mecca (Bus Via del Corso), and **Via Salaria,** a smaller shopping strip (Bus/Tram Via Salaria).
- The basilica and catacombs of **Sant'Agnese.** Ⓐ Via Nomentana 349, ⓣ 06 861 0840, ⓦ www.santagnese.net, Bus Nomentana
- **Museo d'Arte Contemporanea** (MACRO), a modern art museum housed in a former brewery. Ⓐ Via Reggio Emilia 54, ⓣ 06 67 107 0400, ⓦ www.macro.roma.museum, Bus Via Nomentana, Porta Pia

PIAZZA NAVONA/PANTHEON
Bus: **Piazza Navona, Pantheon**

Although this area is a big tourist destination, locals know it as a great place to shop for vintage clothing and used books and music. Restaurants tend to be expensive because of the tourist traffic, but affordable wine bars are popping up on almost every corner. The Pantheon is an architectural marvel for its perfect symmetry, and you'll never lack for spectacles: The Piazza Navona, in particular, may sometimes seem like a human circus.

WHAT YOU'LL SEE:

- Baroque masterpieces by Gianlorenzo Bernini and Francesco Borromini in the middle of **Piazza Navona.** Bus Piazza Navona
- Borromini's staggering **Chiesa di Sant'Ivo alla Sapienza,** built into the courtyard of the original site of Rome's first university. Ⓐ Corso del Rinascimento 40, ⓣ 06 686 4987, Bus Corso del Rinascimento
- Fabulous shoe stores on the streets heading north from the **Pantheon.** Bus Pantheon
- Three stunning Caravaggio paintings inside the sixteenth-century **Chiesa di San Luigi dei Francesi.** Ⓐ Piazza San Luigi dei Francesi, ⓣ 06 68 8271, Bus Corso del Rinascimento

THE SPANISH STEPS/VIA VITTORIO VENETO/PARIOLI
Metro: **Spagna, Barberini, Flaminio**

This area is where the wealthy live, lounge, and spend excessive amounts of money. The neighborhood is also a lovely place to stroll, whether down the Via dei Condotti to window-shop the designer stores (and to glimpse the beautiful salespeople inside) or up the Via Corso to see the charming Piazza del Popolo. Taking the Via del Corso in the opposite direction will land you at Palazzo Venezia, now an art museum, where Mussolini had his offices (and cavorted with his mistress).

WHAT YOU'LL SEE:

- The creepy Capuchin crypts of **Chiesa di Santa Maria della Concezione.** Ⓐ Via Veneto 27, ⊕ 06 487 1185, Ⓜ Barberini
- The begging (or stealing) gypsies, persistent postcard vendors, and horse-drawn carriages that give the **Spanish Steps** a spirit all their own. Ⓜ Spagna
- The **Via Margutta,** once home to legendary filmmaker Federico Fellini, and its numerous art studios, galleries, and shops. Ⓜ Flaminio
- **Piazza Barberini's** terrifically odd mix of the stunning (Palazzo Barberini up the hill) and the grotesque (the flamboyant cinema on the square). Ⓜ Barberini
- Celebrities emerging from the swanky hotels of Via Sistina and Via Vittorio Veneto. Ⓜ Barberini
- The *three* St. Mary's churches in **Piazza del Popolo:** Chiesa di Santa Maria del Popolo, Chiesa di Santa Maria dei Miracoli, and Chiesa di Santa Maria in Montesanto. Ⓜ Flaminio
- **Via Vittorio Veneto,** the setting and inspiration for both the film and the phrase *la dolce vita* (the good life). Ⓜ Barberini
- **Villa Borghese,** an enormous park with a zoo, an art museum, a well-groomed garden, and an impressive palace. Ⓜ Spagna, Flaminio

STAZIONE TERMINI/SAN LORENZO
Metro: Termini, Repubblica

Stazione Termini is Rome's main train station and an important hub for travelers and locals alike, but its notoriously seedy neighborhood is the least safe in the city. The ungentrified San Lorenzo, just next door, is popular among students for its affordable rent and for its all-night bars and cafes.

WHAT YOU'LL SEE:

- The **Teatro dell'Opera di Roma,** Rome's leading Opera House. ⓐ Piazza Beniamino Gigli 8, ⓣ 06 48 1601, ⓦ www.opera.roma.it, Ⓜ Repubblica

- The **Terme di Diocleziano,** ancient baths converted by Michelangelo into a church, the Santa Maria degli Angeli. ⓐ Piazza della Repubblica, ⓣ 06 488 0812, Ⓜ Repubblica

- The **Parco dei Caduti** (Park of the Fallen), with a monument commemorating the horrific Allied bombing of San Lorenzo in 1943. Bus Via Tiburtina

- The *Ecstasy of Santa Teresa,* Bernini's famous sculpture, located in the **Chiesa di Santa Maria della Vittoria.** ⓐ Via XX Settembre 17, ⓣ 06 482 6190, Ⓜ Repubblica

TESTACCIO
Metro: Piramide

This out-of-the-way, gentrifying neighborhood is club central. No matter what your musical preference—world, punk, rap, hip-hop, pop—Testaccio has a venue to match, perhaps because its large, warehouse-type spaces go for low rents. Because it doesn't have many tourist attractions, Testaccio is also a good place to do your weekly food shopping.

WHAT YOU'LL SEE:

- Piazza Testaccio's open-air market, considered the city's biggest. Ⓜ Piramide

- The **pyramid tomb of Caio Cestio,** a wealthy Roman who ordered that his slaves be freed after his death (they built it for him after he died in 12 B.C.E.). Ⓐ Piazza di Porto di San Paolo, Ⓜ Piramide

- The grand **Cimitero Acattolico per gli Stranieri** (Non-Catholic Cemetery for Foreigners), eternal home to Keats and Shelley, among others. Ⓐ Via Caio Cestio 6, Ⓣ 06 574 1900, Ⓜ Piramide

- A lovely walk up the **Aventine Hill,** which offers terrific views of Rome. Bus Via Santa Maria in Cosmedin

- The **Piazza dei Cavalieri di Malta** (Palace of the Knights of Malta), where you can sneak a view of St Peter's Basilica through a keyhole. Ⓐ Piazza Cavalieri di Malta 3, Ⓣ 06 6758 1234, Ⓜ Piramide

TRASTEVERE
Bus: **Piazza Sonnino**

The center of life for many foreigners, Trastevere is a neighborhood in which you're likely to hear English more often than Italian. Pubs, bars, and restaurants line the streets, attracting young people from all over the city. Everywhere you go, you'll notice young beggars holding sleeping puppies designed to break your heart and open your wallet, as well as many American tourists.

WHAT YOU'LL SEE:

- **Janiculum Hill** (not one of the famous seven), where you'll find series of staircases and the stunning Piazzale Giuseppe Garibaldi. Bus Passeggiata del Gianicolo

- **Ponte Sisto,** Rome's most beautiful bridge, built in the fifteenth century. Bus Lungotevere dei Vallati

- **Basilica di Santa Maria in Trastevere,** one of Rome's oldest churches, thought to be the first dedicated to Mary and the first in which mass was openly celebrated. Ⓐ Piazza Santa Maria in Trastevere, Ⓣ 06 581 4802, Bus/Tram Viale Trastevere

- **Alcazar,** a theater that shows American movies in English on Monday nights. Ⓐ Via Merry del Val 14, Ⓣ 06 588 0099, Bus/Tram Viale di Trastevere

- **Porta Portese,** a lively Sunday-morning flea market— both overwhelming and a popular place for pickpockets. Ⓐ Via Portuense at Vi Nippolito Nievo, Bus Porta Portese

- **Museo di Roma,** a folklore museum with great Roman-interest exhibits. Ⓐ Piazza San Pantaleo 10, Ⓣ 06 8207 7304, Ⓦ www.museodiroma.comune.roma.it, Bus Corso Vittorio Emanuele II

VATICAN CITY
Metro: **Cipro–Musei Vaticani**

From profane Trastevere, it's a short trek across the Tiber River to Vatican City, the sacred religious capital of both Catholic Italy and the Catholic world. Technically a city-state unto itself, the Vatican is a walled compound that houses St Peter's Basilica, the Vatican Museums, and the pope's residence and offices. Catholics and non-Catholics alike will find the museum's artistic treasures—including, of course, Michelangelo's famous ceiling in the Sistine Chapel—to be astounding. Once you've had your fill of art, you can enjoy the area's many shops and restaurants.

WHAT YOU'LL SEE:

- **St Peter's Basilica,** featuring Michelangelo's famous sculpture Pieta. Ⓜ Cipro–Musei Vaticani

- The **Sistine Chapel,** which is much smaller than you would probably imagine—but still worth braving the crowds for. Ⓜ Cipro–Musei Vaticani

- **Piazza San Pietro,** where you might see crowds of pilgrims chanting, "Benedetto, Benedetto!" for Pope Bendict XVI.
- The spectacular view of St Peter's from **Via della Concilazione,** cleared by fascist city planners in the 1930s. Bus Via della Concilazione
- **Castel Sant'Angelo,** the mausoleum of the great Emperor Hadrian. Bus Piazza Pia

5 PLACES WHERE YOU'LL FIND AMERICAN STUDENTS

1. **Campo de' Fiori:** The only question is, wine bar, restaurant, or *gelateria* (ice cream parlor)? American students frequent them all—and you will too. Bus Campo de' Fiori

2. **Bar Gli Archi:** A trusted haunt for study-weary students seeking a break, this Monteverde bar is located just up the street from the American University of Rome, at the corner of Vias Fratelli Bonnet and Carini. Ⓐ Via Fratelli Bonnet 4, Ⓣ 06 580 3891, Bus Via Carini, Via Bonnet

3. **Trastevere:** You'll spot American students everywhere in this neighborhood, which not only has numerous pubs, but is also home to the four-year American school John Cabot University. Bus Piazza Sonnino

4. **Abbey Theatre Irish Pub:** You'll feel right at home here, especially during American football season, when you can cheer (in English!) for all your favorite teams. Ⓐ Via del Governo Vecchio 51, 53, Ⓣ 06 686 1341, Ⓦ www.abbey-rome.com, Bus Chiesa Nuova

5. **American movies:** You won't be the only one checking out the latest blockbuster in English. Find films in v.o. (original version) by searching newspaper listings, then enjoy getting all the subtle jokes and cultural references— nuances difficult to catch in any language but your own.

3. Getting Around

The most efficient and cost-effective means of transportation in Rome is the extensive bus and tram network, which provides reliable service throughout the city center and suburbs. Rome's two-line metro system is not as extensive, but it does deliver reliable service to stops within walking distance of all the major sites in the city center.

Roman taxis are expensive, and locals rarely take them. Walking, an excellent way to see the city, is a better alternative. Be forewarned, however, that walking in Rome is not for the faint of heart. Streets are winding and narrow, with sidewalks often barely wide enough for one person. If you think using the alleys will cut down on traffic hazards, think again: Vespas and super-tiny Smart cars can squeeze down even the smallest streets, and their speed will in no way suffer for lack of space. Walk defensively—and get out of the way. Sharing the roads gracefully is a quintessentially Roman challenge.

METRO

Rome's metro is remarkably efficient, considering that it has only two major lines (they cross at Stazione Termini, the city's main train station). One of the biggest controversies in local government centers on the expansion of the metro service. Modern Rome is built on ancient ruins: Whenever the City Council approves construction of new metro lines, builders often inadvertently discover relics of great historical importance that must be either destroyed or built around. The decision almost always goes in favor of historic preservation, hence the system's limited range.

The upside to the system's limited scope is its efficient schedule. Trains run every 7 to 10 minutes during peak hours (5:30 A.M.–11:30 P.M.), and there are rarely delays. Both metro lines run at reduced capacity (every 20 to 30 minutes) from 11:30 P.M. to 1:00 A.M. The metro is closed from 1:00 A.M. to 5:30 A.M. All public transportation in Rome is run by ATAC. For up-to-date maps and fare information, visit ATAC's helpful website, www.atac.roma.it.

NAVIGATING THE SYSTEM

Metro entrances are indicated aboveground with red and white signs marked *M*. Each stop on the line is listed on large, color-coded maps placed at the entrances to the tracks and inside the trains. If you need assistance, most conductors speak English, and fellow passengers are almost always willing to help as well.

To figure out how to get where you're going on the metro, ask yourself three questions:

1. *Where am I going?* Identify the station nearest your destination.

2. *Which line(s) will take me there?* You only have two choices: Line A or Line B. If your destination is on Line B and you're close to a stop on Line A, change trains at Stazione Termini, where the lines meet (or walk to the nearest stop on the line you need).

3. *In which direction am I traveling?* Each metro line goes in only two directions. Line A goes toward either Valle Aurelia or Anagnina. Line B goes toward either Laurentina or Rebibbia. (At Stazione Termini, the main transfer station, you can catch either line.) Use the metro map to identify the end-station you're heading toward, then follow the

station signs for the train going in your desired direction. For example, if you're at the Manzoni stop on Line A and you want to go to Barberini, you'll go in the direction of Valle Aurelia.

BUYING TICKETS

Tickets for trams, buses, and the metro are interchangeable. They can be purchased at *tabacchi* (tobacco shops), bars, and vending machines in the stations. The vending machines accept cash and credit cards; they also offer instructions in English. If you'll be using public transportation regularly, invest in a long-term pass. Depending on your needs, you can get a one-week or a one-month pass, which you can use as often as you like during the specified time period. Choose from the following options.

Individual ride (BIT) The BIT costs €1 and is valid for 75 minutes after the first use. This means you can ride more than once, as long as your travel occurs within that 75-minute period. A 5BIT, the equivalent of five BIT tickets, is also available.

One-day unlimited (BIG) The BIG offers unlimited rides for one day and costs €4. It expires at midnight on the day you use it.

Three-day unlimited (BTI) The BTI gives you unlimited travel for three consecutive days and costs €11. It expires at midnight on the third day.

One-week unlimited (CIS) The CIS gives you unlimited travel for seven consecutive days and costs €16. It expires at midnight on the seventh day.

Monthly A personal pass, which gives you unlimited travel within one calendar month, costs €30 and can be used only by you (carry your ID with you to present to transportation personnel if requested). An anonymous pass, which can be used by more than one person, costs €46. Monthly passes are valid for one calendar month starting on the first day. If you buy a monthly pass mid-month, you'll pay the full price but will be able to use the pass for only part of the month.

STUDENT DISCOUNTS

Discounted monthly passes (€18, normally €30) are available with proper ID—but technically these are only for Italian students who live in Rome. Student passes can be purchased at metro stations where attendants are on duty; try Stazione Termini. As an American student studying abroad, you'll likely have to pay the full fare, but it doesn't hurt to try your luck in finding a lenient attendant.

BUSES AND TRAMS

Buses and trams don't operate on a timed schedule, but they arrive frequently. You rarely have to wait longer than 10 minutes for one, except on Sundays and holidays, when service is more sporadic and the wait can be 30 to 45 minutes. Reduced night service (arriving approximately every hour) runs from 11:30 P.M. to 1:00 A.M. Although regular buses and trams don't run from 1:00 A.M. to 5:00 A.M., you can take a *bus notturno* (night bus) for the same fare as a regular bus. For all bus and tram information, visit ATAC's website, www.atac.roma.it.

NAVIGATING THE SYSTEM

At every bus stop, you'll find a yellow sign that lists arriving bus lines and the stops along each, arranged in easy-to-read columns. To figure out what bus to take, first identify your stop, then identify the last stop on that bus line. This last stop will appear on an electronic banner on the front of the bus. Navigating the tram system involves the same steps. Bus tickets may be purchased before boarding or from the driver; tram tickets must be purchased before boarding.

Board a bus through the front or back doors and exit from the middle doors. As soon as you board, find the validation machine (it will be yellow or red), usually located in the back of a bus and throughout the cars of a tram. If you have a single-ride, one-day, three-day, or weekly ticket, validate it here. You don't need to validate a monthly ticket, but be sure to have it with you, along with your ID. To exit the bus, ring one of the buzzers—you'll see them throughout the bus—right before it reaches your stop; otherwise, the driver may skip it.

STAYING SAFE

In general, you'll find traveling by public transportation to be perfectly safe in Rome. If you do have a problem, it will probably be a matter of pickpocketing or mugging (though mugging occurs rarely). Try to board cars that are moderately full of passengers and keep your valuables close to you at all times.

TAXIS

Because of air and noise pollution, some parts of the city center are closed to all but local car traffic during the day. Taxis, however, are allowed in all parts of the city center at all times. There are surprisingly few taxi stands in central Rome, and hailing a cab is almost impossible. If you need a taxi, seek the help of a hotel valet (don't forget to tip).

If you can't find a taxi, the flat-rate car services listed here are reliable. Fares are negotiable, but be sure to agree on a price before you get in. Know, too, that the meter starts running when you place the call, not when the taxi reaches you. Roman taxis are expensive, but they're safe—even though some drivers feel free to go down one-way streets in the wrong direction.

- **Pronto Taxi** Ⓣ 06 6645
- **Radio Taxi 3570** Ⓣ 06 3570, Ⓦ www.3570.it

TAXI FARES

The base taxi fare is €2.33 from 7:00 A.M. to 10:00 P.M., Monday to Saturday. After 10:00 P.M. and on weekends and holidays, the base fare jumps to €3.36. Each kilometer costs €0.78, and during peak traffic times (or at speeds of less than 20 km per hour), the fare is metered in increments of 10.2 seconds. If you have luggage, you'll be charged about €1 for each piece. Pay the driver in cash at the end of the ride. Some cab companies accept credit cards, but this needs to be negotiated in advance. The standard tip for a metered cab ride is 10 to 15 percent. If you have a lot of luggage and the driver helps you load and unload it (a common practice), consider upping the tip a bit.

BIKES

Biking is not the safest form of transportation in Rome, thanks to the traffic congestion and the aggressiveness (or craziness) of Roman drivers. Biking can, however, be pleasant in quiet neighborhoods such as Janiculum Hill, Testaccio, and San Lorenzo. Also lovely are rides down the Appian Way (the old Roman road) and out to and around the catacombs. Few Romans use bikes as their only means of transportation in the city.

New bikes range in price from €75 to €2,500, depending on the brand and the style. All of the major brands common in the United States, including Trek, Univega, and Schwinn, are available in Italy, along with several Italian brands, such as Ablocco and Bianchi. If you're interested in buying a new bike, you can start with Lazzaretti or St Peter Moto, both of which have English-speaking staff. To buy a used bike, check out Scooter for Rent.

Lazzaretti Ⓐ Piazza Fiume 4, Ⓣ 06 855 3828, Ⓜ Castro Pretorio

St Peter Moto Ⓐ Via di Porta Castello 43, Ⓣ 06 575 7063, Bus Via Casilina

Scooter for Rent Ⓐ Via della Purificazione 84, Ⓣ 06 488 5485, Ⓜ Barberini

RENTING A BIKE

Plenty of places in Rome will rent you a bike for several hours or a day. Hourly charges are about €5, while daily rentals are in the €10–€15 range. Here are two rental shops located near Stazione Termini.

Eco Move Rent Ⓐ Via Varese 48–50, Ⓣ 06 4470 4518, Ⓦ www.ecomoverent.com, Ⓜ Termini

Treno e Scooter Rent Ⓐ Stazione Termini, Ⓣ 06 488 2797, Ⓜ Termini

GENERAL RULES OF THE ROAD FOR CYCLISTS

Contrary to what you might expect, cyclists in Rome don't have the right-of-way over cars. The smartest way to ride is defensively. Here are a few key points to keep in mind:

- **Safety:** Always wear a helmet. It's the law, and the protection will give you a measure of safety in the chaos that is Roman traffic.

- **Required equipment:** If you ride your bike after sunset, using a headlight is required by law.

- **Where you can bike:** Biking is legally permitted anywhere in the city, but it's not safe to bike through major roundabouts such as Piazza Venezia or Piazza del Popolo. Take side streets instead.

CARS AND SCOOTERS

Driving a car in Italy is a notoriously hair-raising experience. Roads tend to have only one lane in each direction, and drivers pass routinely, even on curves. Even on the *autostrade* (the Italian version of freeways), which have at least two lanes going in either direction, drivers invariably pass on the left while remaining partially in the right lane. To say the least, the practice takes some getting used to. Scooters and motorbikes are a popular mode of transportation for many young people, probably because they're the perfect size for navigating Rome's often perplexing streets and alleys.

As a student, you'll probably have to do very little driving while you're abroad. If you're set on exploring Rome or Italy from behind the wheel, see "Renting a Car" in Chapter 17.

GENERAL RULES OF THE ROAD FOR DRIVERS

For the most part, the same rules you'd follow in the United States apply in Rome. Here are a few reminders:

- **Turn signals:** A blinking turn signal can mean someone is either turning *or* passing, so don't pass until you're sure of what the other car is doing.

- **Safety:** Wearing a seatbelt is mandatory by law, but hardly anyone does it (despite stiff fines).

- **Cell phones:** Using a cell phone while driving is illegal unless you have a hands-free device.

- **Speed:** If you're driving too slowly, drivers behind you will flash their lights. If you're uncomfortable with Roman drivers' sometimes shocking speeds, make sure you stay to the right.

- **Gas stations:** Most gas stations close from 12:30 P.M. to 3:00 P.M. for lunch, but you can sometimes find a self-service station that allows you to pump your own gas at any time. Some stations take cash only.

TRAINS

The Italian train system, run by Trenitalia, will take you almost anywhere you want to go in the country. Trains in Italy are categorized by speed, level of comfort, and number of stops made on the way to your destination. If your destination is a large city, consider taking the Eurostar or InterCity rather than the local trains. The high-speed trains may cost more, but they are more comfortable and don't stop as frequently. While most local trains don't have reserved seating, Eurostar reservations include seat assignments and InterCity trains offer seat assignments for an extra €3. The additional charge is generally worthwhile, especially if you're traveling with others and would like to sit together.

Most trains leave Rome from Stazione Termini. Be aware that track information is sometimes unavailable until 5 to 10 minutes before your train's arrival. While you're waiting, validate your ticket in one of the machines located at the head of the platform. (If you forget, the conductor will validate your ticket on board for a fee; the amount depends on your destination.) You can buy train tickets online or in person at Stazione Termini; cash or credit cards are accepted. For information about destinations, schedules, and fares for both local and high-speed trains, visit Trenitalia's detailed website, available in English, at www.trenitalia.com.

TO AND FROM THE AIRPORTS

Rome is served primarily by Leonardo da Vinci Fiumicino Airport (FCO), located about 16 miles outside of the city. Ciampino (CIA), a smaller airport often used by low-cost airlines, is situated approximately 10 miles from Rome. You can reach both airports by public transportation.

TO/FROM FCO

Trenitalia Trenitalia offers high-speed service from Stazione Termini to FCO (and vice versa) every 30 minutes from 5:30 A.M. to 11:00 P.M. The price is €9.50, and the trip is approximately 35 minutes long.

Cab/car service Taking a taxi between FCO and the city center costs about €50–€75 and takes about 45 minutes.

TO/FROM CIA

Cab/car service Taking a taxi between CIA and the city center costs approximately €20–€25 and takes about 20 minutes.

Shuttle buses EasyJet and Ryanair both offer shuttle buses between CIA and Stazione Termini for about €8 one way; the trip takes approximately 30 minutes.

City buses City buses run between CIA and the metro stop Anagnina (on Line A) and between CIA and the Ciampino train station. To continue into the city center, you'll have to take the metro from Anagnina (€1) or the train from Ciampino (around €2). Although cheaper than shuttle buses, city buses are more of a hassle: They are often crowded, with little room for luggage, and taking them requires that you make a transfer. The total trip takes approximately 30 minutes.

TRAVELERS WITH DISABILITIES

Unfortunately, Rome's hilly terrain makes getting around particularly challenging for those with disabilities. Trains, railway stations, buses, trams, major sites, and many restaurants are usually equipped for wheelchairs, but only some metro stations are accessible. Check out www.accessible-italy.com, www.initaly.com/travel/handicap.htm, and www.italiaplease.com for more information on all aspects of everyday life for people with disabilities.

5 THINGS THAT WILL MAKE YOU THINK, "NOW *THAT'S* ROME"

1. **Line cutting:** Romans tend to have a me-first mentality when it comes to being served.

2. **Canine "surprises" on the sidewalks:** It's true that Rome offers more towering architectural surprises than practically any other city, but don't forget to look down every so often. Stepping on dog waste is a quintessential Roman experience, especially for out-of-towners who don't know better.

3. **Roman chic:** If it's a sunny day, the locals will look sharp in their crisp tailored suits, while you sweat from every pore in your shorts and t-shirt. And if it's raining, they'll easily navigate the slippery cobblestone streets in four-inch heels, while you slip and fall in sneakers. Try as you might, you probably will never pass for an Italian.

4. **Unwanted advances:** Though they're generally harmless, young Italian males will occasionally live up to their reputations as devastatingly charming, sweep-you-off-your-feet Romeos.

5. **Adventures in public transportation:** The bus ride that took 10 minutes yesterday? It takes 45 minutes today. Between rush-hour traffic, transportation strikes, and general inconsistency, traveling across Rome is always an adventure.

4. Finding Housing

Getting an apartment in Rome is a prospect both thrilling and daunting. You can start your apartment search before you leave the United States by checking the Internet's plentiful resources—if you want, you can even secure a place before seeing it in person. However, if you can arrange for short-term accommodation upon arriving in Rome, even for just a week or two, your chances of finding a place you love will be even greater. After all, online pictures will never reveal an apartment's street noise or rude neighbors.

Sharing an apartment with a roommate or two is a common practice among young people in Rome, although apartments tend to be quite small. (Larger apartments are generally out of a student's price range.) Italian rentals are almost always unfurnished—many won't even have basic appliances such as refrigerators. What Roman apartments lack in modern amenities, however, is more than made up for in charm and character.

APARTMENT LISTINGS

The cheapest way to find an apartment in Rome is to do it yourself, without the help of a broker or third-party agent. Be quick in responding to ads, and don't shy away from being persistent or making early-morning phone calls. Online listings tend to be more up to date and more useful—search the print publications only when they are hot off the presses.

Many Italian real-estate websites are geared toward Americans and are therefore written in English. The English Yellow Pages (www.intoitaly.it), Craigslist Rome (http://rome.craigslist.org), and www.sublet.com are all good resources. You can also peruse local newspapers, such as the English-language *Wanted in Rome* (www.wantedinrome.com), published every two weeks, and *Porta Portese* (www.portaportese.it), which consists almost entirely of classified ads and comes out twice weekly.

APARTMENT HUNTING TIPS

Here are a few key points to keep in mind during you apartment search:

- If you're looking for a *parte dell'appartamento* (apartment share), seek out ads that specifically mention sharing. You can often find notices posted by people seeking a *compagno di camera* (roommate) on university bulletin boards.

- Apartment ads will almost always include monthly price, number of bedrooms and bathrooms, and spatial measurements. But remember that Italians use the metric system: Measurements will be in square meters, not square feet.

- Make sure you ask for the physical address when you call or email in response to an ad. Ad writers may exaggerate or omit certain details: An apartment listed as being in Trastevere, for example, might be in the epicenter of the lively neighborhood—or it might be across the tram tracks in the seedy post-war architecture section.

- Bring a checklist with you when you visit prospective apartments. Be sure to check for things such as storage space, electrical outlets, water pressure, whether you can hear noise from the street or neighboring apartments, and whether appliances such as the refrigerator and stove are in good working order.

APARTMENT LISTING LEXICON

Floors in Rome are numbered differently than they are in the United States. The ground floor is called the *piano terra* and the *primo piano* (first floor) is one level up. To reach the *terzo piano* (third floor), you will have to climb three (not two) sets of stairs. Here are some other common terms you'll find in apartment ads:

affittasi	for rent
arredata	furnished
aria condizionata	air-conditioning
ascensore	elevator
bagno	bathroom
camera da letto	bedroom
cucina abitabile	eat-in kitchen
cucinotto	small or efficiency kitchen
giardino	garden
monolocale	studio
non ammobiliato	unfurnished
parzialmente arredati	partly furnished
soggiorno	den, living room
vendesi	for sale
vuoto	empty (no furniture or kitchen)

BROKERS

A broker will facilitate your search and handle the negotiations with prospective landlords. The catch, of course, is that you'll have to pay a broker's fee, usually equal to a month's rent or 10 percent of a year's rent. You may be hit with additional fees if your broker takes care of setting up the utilities (gas, electricity, and telephone).

An added benefit of using brokers is that they may be able to help you obtain certain documents required by the government, such as a *permesso di soggiorno* (visitor's permit; see "Student Visas" in Chapter 1) and a fiscal (tax) code. Italian bureaucracy is famously difficult to navigate: The expert assistance alone could justify the money you'll spend on a broker's fees.

Don't be shy about working with more than one broker if you want to, as the practice is not frowned upon in Italy. You can begin your search with these two agencies.

At Home Ⓐ Via del Babuino 56, Ⓣ 06 3212 0102, Ⓦ www.at-home-italy.com, Ⓜ Spagna

Rome Power Ⓐ Via Paolo Emilio 7, Ⓣ 06 3211 0998, Ⓦ www.romepower.com, Ⓜ Lepanto

APARTMENT PRICES

When you rent an apartment, be prepared to pay up to three months' rent before moving in: the first month's rent and a security deposit equivalent to one or two months' rent. (The security deposit will be refunded upon your departure, assuming you leave the place in decent condition.) If you go through an agency, the broker's fee will add to your expenses, bringing the upfront total to four months' rent—sometimes more.

On average, long-term (over six months) rentals in the more affordable neighborhoods begin at about €500 a month for a studio with a kitchenette and a bathroom, €1,000 a month for a one-bedroom apartment with a full kitchen and bathroom, and €1,800 a month for a two-bedroom apartment with a full kitchen and bathroom. Prices go up with location, view, and amenities (such as terraces and furniture). The most expensive neighborhoods are the Spanish Steps, Parioli, and Trastevere. More affordable areas include San Lorenzo, Esquiline, and Nomentano.

LOCATION, LOCATION, LOCATION

Aside from the more upscale areas, you'll find students living all over Rome. San Lorenzo is a particularly student-friendly area. Here are rough estimates of what you'll pay per month for an unfurnished studio or one-bedroom apartment in some of the most popular neighborhoods.

- The Spanish Steps: €1,000/€1,800
- Trastevere: €1,000/€1,800
- Parioli: €800/€1,600
- San Lorenzo: €500/€1,000
- Esquiline: €650/€1,200
- Nomentano: €500/€1,000

LEASES

You may be forced to make a fast decision when looking at an apartment, as there is rarely any shortage of potential renters. Do not, however, sign a lease or hand over any money if you have lingering doubts. Once you sign a lease, you'll have a difficult time getting out of your obligations or being reimbursed. Unfortunately, Italian law doesn't protect renters adequately. Take steps to protect yourself before committing to a place—including asking your landlords for references, if possible, or requesting to talk to current tenants.

UNDERSTANDING LEASES

Many landlords will accept lease agreements of six months, although they'll probably want you to stay for a minimum of one year. Most Italian leases do not expressly forbid subletting: If you need to move out early, finding somebody to take your place could be an option. Expect a standard lease to include the following information:

- The rental period and starting date

- The amount of rent, when it's due, and how it should be paid—many landlords prefer standing orders (that is, direct debits from a bank account) as opposed to checks

- Penalties for late payment

- What utilities are included

- Who is responsible for repairs and any other responsibilities the landlord has to the tenant (such as bill payment)

- The amount of the security deposit, who will hold it (typically the landlord or the company that manages the property), and what rate of interest it will earn

HOMESTAYS

A homestay is a semester- or yearlong arrangement in which you live with an Italian family—typically with your own bedroom, a bathroom that may or may not be shared, and two meals a day. The advantage to a homestay is that it forces you to immerse yourself in the language and culture, something that is difficult to do if you're living in a studio apartment or a student residence.

Before you decide that a homestay is for you, be careful to assess your eating preferences. Meals can be hit or miss depending on your host's culinary skills (and your level of pickiness). Refusing meals may create friction in the household. And because board is included in the price of a homestay, you'll wind up paying double if you feel the need to eat out frequently. If you have any dietary restrictions, such as vegetarianism or allergies, you might need more control over meal preparation than homestays allow.

If you'd like to pursue a homestay, discuss this option with your school. Your program might be able to match you with an Italian family, or you can try combing apartment listings for homestay notices. Families will often advertise rooms specifically intended for young international students. Rates for homestays vary depending on the specific accommodations that you or your school arrange.

5 ROMAN APARTMENT QUIRKS

1. **Complicated elevators:** To get in and out of your elevator, you'll likely have to push open two or three different sets of doors—an especially challenging task if you're balancing books or shopping bags.

2. **No dryers:** Sure, clothes hanging above the street look charming on postcards, but living in a city devoid of dryers takes some getting used to. You'll probably have access to a washing machine but not a dryer. Plan accordingly, and expect that your jeans will fit more loosely during your stay.

3. **Gas stoves:** You'll usually need two hands to light your burners—one to control the gas, one to hold a flame.

4. **No microwaves:** You probably won't see many microwaves during your time in Rome—they're just not that common.

5. **Minuscule spaces:** Roman apartments are often space-efficient, meaning incredibly cramped. For instance, bathrooms sometimes don't have separate showers—instead, a showerhead is located above the toilet, and the bathroom *is* the shower stall.

5. Shopping

S hopping, particularly for food, is one of the greatest pleasures of living in Rome. Unlike Americans, Italians don't hold one-stop convenience as a broad cultural value. Even the younger generations prefer to buy their fruit at a fruit market, meat at a meat market, and cheese at a cheese market. Fortunately, this process is made more convenient by the presence of small specialty shops in central areas of every neighborhood. Italians don't see shopping for food as a chore. They see it more as a social activity—one that's not relegated exclusively to women.

And for non-food-related shopping, Rome will not disappoint—even if you're on the tightest of student budgets. You may be tempted to browse at one of the city's high-end designer retailers, or to pop into a few cool boutiques as you make your way around town. But to maximize your purchasing power, head straight to one of Rome's excellent flea markets.

SUPERMARKETS

Italian supermarkets are primarily devoted to food, a matter due as much to space limitations as to cultural philosophy. You won't see magazines or newspapers for sale in the supermarkets at all, and you'll find just small sections for cleaning supplies and toiletries (these are better purchased at a superstore or a specialty shop). Supermarkets are generally open from 7:00 A.M. to 9:00 P.M.

Coop is an affordable mainstream supermarket chain that carries both food and household supplies: Its stores are found all over the city and are recognizable by their yellow and brown signs. The only real supermarket in the city center, however, is Supermercati GS: The largest of all the chain supermarkets in Rome, it sells everything from food to automotive supplies and is located at Viale del Galoppatoio, near the entrance to the Villa Borghese.

- **Coop** Various locations Ⓦ www.e-coop.it
- **Supermercati GS** Ⓐ Viale del Galoppatoio, Ⓣ 800 241 241, Ⓦ www.supermercatigs.it, Bus Viale San Paolo del Brasile

GROCERY SHOPPING 101

Keep these tips in mind when you're heading out to the grocery aisles:

- **Buying produce:** Produce must be weighed by a clerk before you take it to the register. There are scales in the produce area, with clerks at the ready.

- **Understanding quantities:** Most Italian products are measured in the metric system. Take note of these conversions: one kilogram = about 2.2 lbs, 100 g = 3.5 oz, and 1 L = 2.1 pints.

- **Buying milk:** You may be surprised to discover that milk is *not* shelved in the refrigerated section like it is in the United States. Shelf-stable milk is popular in Italy and can be stored at room temperature for up to a year: Once opened, it lasts only as long as fresh milk does. All milk sold in grocery stores is pasteurized.

GROCERY SHOPPING LEXICON

Stocking up on groceries? Here are a few choice words you'll encounter in a grocery store:

burro	butter
cipolla	onion
latte	milk
lattuga	lettuce
maiale	pork
manzo	beef
olio	oil
oliva	olive
pane	bread
pesce	fish
pomodoro	tomato
sale	salt
uovo	egg
zucchero	sugar

SPECIALTY FOODS

Italians are justifiably proud of their national and regional cuisines. You'll find innumerable *negozi del formaggio* (cheese shops), *pasticcerie* (pastry shops), *panetterie* (bread bakeries), and *macellerie* (butcher shops). Health and organic food shops have also become popular, as have shops catering to specialty cooking—ranging from Latin American to African— once unheard of in traditional Roman kitchens.

BAKERIES

Bakeries in Rome fall into two categories: *pasticcerie* (those specializing primarily in sweet baked goods) and *panetterie* (those specializing primarily in bread). Popular local sweets include *biscotti* (long, twice-baked cookies), *panettoni* (cakes loaded with dried fruits and nuts), and *cornetti* (rolls filled with custard or jam). Savory specialties commonly available are pizza by the square, spinach-stuffed crepes and calzones, and, of course, all manner of bread. Most bakeries remain closed after the mid-day siesta.

CHEESE SHOPS

Most stores that focus on high-quality cheeses also sell cured meats, olives, and some canned goods, such as tuna from Italy's long coastline. The most popular local cheese is *pecorino romano,* a cousin of the *pecorino* (sheep's-milk cheese) that is the pride of Sardinia. The best place in all of Rome to sample and buy cheeses, in small or large quantity, is the high-end Italian grocery store Volpetti, in Testaccio.

Volpetti Ⓐ Via Marmorata 47, Ⓣ 06 574 2352, Ⓦ www.volpetti.com, Ⓜ Piramide

SAY CHEESE!

Fontina is a medium-hard cheese from the north-west region of the Valle d'Aosta that's especially good for melting. *Gorgonzol* is a blue cheese from Italy's Po Valley. *Parmigiano Reggiano* and *Grana Padano* are the two most-revered cheeses made in the grana style—that is, finely grained and hard. *Mascarpone* is a super-soft cheese from Lombardy that's used in desserts. *Mozzarella*, of course , is delectable on its own or in all manner of pasta, pizza, and other dishes.

BUTCHERS

Italian butchers tend to be much more specialized than American butchers; you'll even find pork-only and horse-only butchers. But the majority sell all of the available varieties and cuts of meat, many of which you may not be used to. For example, while American butchers sell the whole leg of a lamb, Italian butchers cut it into the lower-leg portion and the saddle—and they sell the head, feet, and neck for stews. Little is wasted. The same is true for veal, which is more commonly consumed in Italy than in the United States. Arguably the best butcher in Rome is Annibale, which has been in business for more than 100 years.

Annibale Ⓐ Via di Ripetta 236/237, Ⓣ 06 361 2269, Ⓜ Spagna

FISHMONGERS

Eating fish on Fridays is the rule in this Catholic country, and almost all restaurants offer fish specials on that day. Fish markets do their briskest business on Fridays because Italians almost invariably eat their fish on the day of purchase. You'll find calamari in Italian fish shops, as well as octopus and *seppia* (cuttlefish). And while Americans tend to eat only fillets, Italians are prone to eating the whole fish, either grilled or fried.

FARMERS' MARKETS

Italy's outdoor markets are deservedly world famous for quality and price, and Rome has some of the country's best. The atmosphere is just as important as the food: At a farmers' market, the romantic idea of *la dolce vita* really lives up to its promise. Stroll around the stalls before committing to a vendor. Chat about sources if you speak a little Italian. Some vendors grow their own produce, and some offer organic food. Farmers' markets are not for produce alone: Most also offer meats and cheeses; a few even sell livestock.

Most neighborhoods have at least one farmers' market, usually open from 7:00 A.M. until 2:00 P.M., Monday through Saturday. Almost all outdoor food markets are closed on Sundays. The markets are of varying sizes, and every one has its own distinctive character and atmosphere, depending on the clientele and the neighborhood. Here are a few of the most popular markets in Rome.

Campo de' Fiori Rome's most famous market offers fruit, vegetables (many of them organic), local olive oils, and other ingredients for discerning cooks. It's surrounded by beautiful outdoor cafes, so pop in for an espresso between shopping rounds. Ⓐ Piazza Campo de' Fiori, Bus Campo de' Fiori

Piazza Vittorio Market Rome's first ethnic market offers a multicultural shopping experience. You'll mingle with Chinese, Vietnamese, and African home cooks and restaurant chefs. Ⓐ Piazza Vittorio (near Stazione Termini), Ⓜ Stazione Termini

Testaccio Market There's nary a tourist in sight at Rome's largest outdoor market, favored by serious local home cooks as well as chefs from many neighborhood restaurants. You'll have difficulty seeing it all—but if you have time, you can find absolutely anything you might be looking for. Ⓐ Via Marmorata (near Volpetti in the Piramide neighborhood), Ⓜ Piramide

Trastevere Market Much like the Campo de' Fiori market, but smaller and more manageable, this market mostly sells organic fruits and vegetables, along with handmade crafts. Ⓐ Piazza San Cosimato, Bus Piazza Sonnino

Trifonale Food and Flower Market This neighborhood market is best known for its variety of well-priced, high-quality flowers, but the produce is also excellent. Ⓐ Piazza Trifonale (in the Prati neighborhood), Ⓜ Piazza di Spagna

SPECIAL DIETS

If you're a vegetarian, you'll find plenty of fresh produce at Rome's farmers' markets. The most popular vegan/vegetarian resource in Rome is a website: Happy Cow (www.happycow.net) tracks vegetarian-friendly restaurants and shops throughout Europe. To find food and groceries for kosher diets, check out the Testaccio Farmers' Market and the Jewish Ghetto, where you'll find some kosher butchers and restaurants. You can find halal food stalls at the food market in the Piazza Vittorio.

FLEA MARKETS

Almost every neighborhood has a Sunday flea market that features inexpensive clothing, household goods, antiques, furniture, hardware, and electronics. Newer specialty markets sell everything from vintage LPs to the latest-model digital cameras. Many local jewelers and other artisans set up tables as well. Here are some of the best flea markets in the city.

Garage Sale, Rigattiere per Hobby Sunday, 10:00 A.M.–7:00 P.M.
Ⓐ Piazzale della Marina, Bus Ostia

Porta Portese Market Sunday, 7:00 A.M.–2:00 P.M.
Ⓐ Via Portuense at Vi Nippolito Nievo, Bus Porta Portese

Underground Monday–Saturday, 10:00 A.M.–2:00 P.M.
Ⓐ Parking Ludovisi, Garage Ludovisi, Ⓜ Spagna.

Via Sannio Market Monday–Saturday, 9:00 A.M.–2:00 P.M.
Ⓐ Piazza Sannio, Bus Villa Celimontana

ONE-STOP SHOPPING

One-stop shopping is a relatively new concept in Rome. All the same, you'll find several places where you can pick up not only any food-related items you need, but also toiletries, household cleaners, and inexpensive clothing such as socks and underwear. Standa, a full-service grocery chain, often places its stores within the larger department stores Oviesse and COIN, creating one-stop-shopping destinations. CONAD, a twenty-four-hour British chain gaining popularity in Italy, is best known for its reasonably priced prepared foods. Supermercati GS is also good for one-stop shopping (see the "Supermarkets" section for contact information).

(see the "Supermarkets" section for contact information)

COIN (with a Standa store inside) Ⓐ Via Cola di Rienzo 173, Ⓣ 06 324 3130, Ⓜ Vaticano

CONAD Ⓐ Stazione Termini 06, Ⓣ 06 667 8400, Ⓜ Stazione Termini; Ⓐ Via Vascherelle 13, Ⓣ 06 669 8481, Ⓜ Spagna

Oviessa (with a Standa store inside) Ⓐ Viale di Trastevere 60, Ⓣ 06 7267 0001, Bus Piazza Sonnino

HOME FURNISHINGS

If you need to pick up a few essential items or if you just want to change your décor, you can furnish your place by shopping at one of the following discount centers (note that Ikea offers home delivery, with charges ranging from €70 to €125).

Euromobilia Centro Europeo del Mobile Ⓐ Via Pontina, Ⓣ 06 910 7610, Tram Via Ponte Vecchia

Ikea Anagnina location: Ⓐ Via delle Vigne 81, Ⓣ 199 11 46 46, Ⓦ www.ikea.it, Ⓜ Anagnina, then Bus #046, 506, or 507 to Ikea; Porta di Roma location: Ⓐ Via delle Vigne Nuove, Ⓣ 199 11 46 46, Ⓦ www.ikea.it, Bus # 38, 84, or 34 to Via Baseggio

Mobilnovo (slightly more expensive, but very high quality)
Ⓐ Via Sicilia 267, Ⓣ 06 4282 7431, Ⓦ www.mobilnovo.it,
Bus Via Aurelia, Tram Vaticano

HIGH-TRAFFIC SHOPPING AREAS

Part of the fun of living in Rome is discovering the
amazing shops that seem to lurk around every corner,
and getting to know the unique stores that are closest
to where you live or study. If you're in the mood for
a shopping spree, head to one of these areas, each of
which offers a staggering selection.

Via del Corso This is Rome's prime shopping artery,
featuring some of the classiest designer names as well
as big-name megastores like Benetton, Diesel, and the
Messaggerie Musicali music store. Ⓜ Spagna or Flaminio

Via dei Condotti, Via Borgognona, Via Frattina Located
between Via del Corso and the Spanish Steps, these parallel
streets boast designers like Armani, Prada, Gucci, Bulgari,
Ferragamo, Valentino, and Hermes. Ⓜ Spagna or Flaminio

Via del Babuino Spanning north to Piazza del Popolo and
parallel to Via del Corso, Via del Babuino is lined with high-
end antique shops and art galleries. Ⓜ Spagna or Flaminio

Via del Governo Vecchio This street in the Centro Storico
is the place to go for cutting-edge fashions, accessories,
and housewares. There are also a few second-hand clothing
shops. Bus Corso Vittorio Emanuele II

Via dei Coronari Located to the northeast of Piazza Navona,
Via dei Coronari is renowned for its high-end antiques—
particularly antique furniture—and art galleries. Bus Corso
del Rinascimento

Via Nazionale and the Trevi Fountain Less jam-packed
and less high-priced than Via del Corso, this area has mid-
range, mainstream clothing stores and leather shops.
Ⓜ Repubblica

Vatican City In addition to pope keychains, pope spoons, and pope postcards, you'll find a variety of fashion boutiques along Via Cola di Rienzo. Ⓜ Ottaviano

5 GREAT GIFTS TO SEND HOME

1. **AS Roma football jersey:** Nothing says *Rome* like an official jersey, especially since Italy's 2006 World Cup victory.

2. **High-end knock offs:** Send a fake Gucci or Prada purse. You'll find vendors set up on blankets all over the city's streets, particularly in tourist-heavy areas such as Vatican City and Campo de' Fiori.

3. **A taste of the old country:** You can't send a restaurant home, but you can send bags of mixed spices from the spice sellers at Campo de' Fiori. Mixed with a little olive oil and drizzled over pasta, the spices transform an ordinary dinner.

4. **Pope paraphernalia:** Even your nonreligious friends will appreciate the staggering array of kitschy pope merchandise for sale.

5. **Italian coffee:** Give your friends a sip of what they're missing by sending coffee from Sant' Eustachio (Ⓐ Piazza Sant-Eustachio 82, ⓣ 06 6880 2048, Bus Largo Torre Argentino) or Tazza D'Oro (Ⓐ Via degli Orfani 84, ⓣ 06 679 2768, Ⓦ www.tazzadorocoffeeshop.com, Bus Largo Torre Argentina), both just steps away from the Pantheon.

LEVATA
ORE

6. Daily Living

Learning to navigate the ins and outs of daily life is part of the game when you're assimilating to a new city. Skills that you take for granted, such as doing laundry, handling money matters, and mailing packages, will suddenly seem new and perplexing. Factor in the linguistic barrier, and even the simplest tasks can become enormous—and often comical— new challenges.

When you deal with service institutions in Rome, several major cultural differences will make themselves apparent. For instance, Romans don't relish waiting in line: At places like small post offices and banks, customers commonly disregard obvious lines and try to slip in front. Knowing what to expect when you tackle day-to-day needs should help you keep your cool.

GETTING MONEY

Before you leave home, set up your U.S. bank and credit card accounts to make them easier to manage from outside the country. Make a point of signing up for online banking and electronic bill payment. Notify your debit- and credit-card providers that you'll be using your cards overseas. Finally, find out how to deposit checks by mail, because you won't be able to make deposits to U.S. bank accounts from Roman ATMs.

GETTING CASH FROM HOME

The fastest and most economical way to get cash from home is to withdraw it from your U.S. account through an ATM. Most U.S. banks place daily (and often weekly) limits on withdrawal amounts. They also charge fees for transactions and currency conversion. Ask your bank for details. Also keep in mind the following options.

- **Wiring money:** You can arrange to have money wired to you from your U.S. bank, but this isn't a good choice if you need the money quickly: Both the sending and receiving banks charge fees, and the transfer can take ten business days or longer.

- **International money transfers:** If you have an Italian bank account, you can have money transferred into your account through an international money transfer. This can take up to forty-eight hours, and you will usually be charged a moderate-to-steep fee.

- **Western Union or American Express:** You'll receive money quickly—within an hour—using either of these services, but the fees are exorbitant. For the nearest locations in Rome, go to www.westernunion.com or www.americanexpress.com.

- **Cash advance:** You can pull cash from your credit card account, but you'll need to make sure you have a PIN number before you leave the United States. Be warned: Interest rates can exceed 25 percent.

- **Cashing U.S. checks:** As a general rule, it's best not to have U.S. checks mailed to you, as you'll have a difficult time finding a Roman bank that will cash them. Your university might have a check-chasing program; inquire at your school.If you have an American Express card, you can cash a personal U.S. check at Rome's American Express office.

CHANGING MONEY

Unfortunately for U.S. travelers, the euro has been worth more than the dollar in recent years. The exchange rate fluctuates constantly, but €1 may cost from about $1.15 to $1.45 (you can easily locate the current exchange rate with a quick online search). If you're on a tight budget, check daily and wait until the rate is as favorable as possible before you withdraw or exchange a large sum of money. Using an ATM to withdraw cash is your best bet for a getting a good exchange rate. Here are some other options if you need to trade dollars for euros or vice versa:

- **Banks:** Most Italian banks will exchange currency for a small commission.

- **Airports:** You will notice exchange booths at the airports, both when you leave the United States and when you arrive in Italy. These booths generally offer very unfavorable rates.

- **Exchange counters:** You can usually find small currency-conversion kiosks at train stations and in touristy neighborhoods (look for signs in English with the word *exchange*). Expect to be charged a high commission.

CREDIT CARDS

MasterCard and Visa are widely accepted in Italy. If you're an American Express user, however, you might want to bring a backup card because Amex is not consistently recognized in Europe. Before you leave the United States, call your credit card companies and let them know you'll be abroad to prevent false alarms about fraudulent charges (and the accompanying hassles of frozen accounts). Ask, also, about the fees you may be charged for overseas credit-card transactions—the industry standard is a 2 to 3 percent finance charge.

ITALIAN BANK ACCOUNTS

You might be able to get by without opening a bank account in Rome—at least for a short period of time. But if you'll be living in Italy for longer than six months, opening a local bank account is probably a good idea. Having an Italian account will not only allow you to deposit any checks you receive (provided they're drafted in euros rather than dollars), it will also help you avoid the charges assessed by U.S. banks for overseas transactions. What's more, if you plan to live in an apartment, you'll most likely need to have a local bank account before you can sign up for utilities (see the "Apartment Living" section).

OPENING AN ACCOUNT

Your school may have a partnership with a specific bank—an option definitely worth considering. If you need to select a bank on your own, you'll find that basic accounts vary little from one institution to another. Many banks offer youth advantages for people under twenty-five. Choose a bank that has a full-service branch near where you live or study. Although you can make withdrawals and deposits at any branch of your bank, you'll have to visit your home bank, which is the bank where you opened your account, to complete any paperwork.

Normal banking hours are 8:45 A.M. to 1:30 P.M. and 2:45 P.M. to 4:00 P.M., Monday through Friday. Some larger branches are open until 6:00 P.M. on Thursdays and from 9:00 A.M. to noon on Saturdays. Some of the most popular banks in Rome are listed on the following page (call or check the website to find the nearest locations).

- **Banca Intesa** Ⓣ 06 67121, Ⓦ www.bancaintesa.it
- **Banca Nazionale del Lavoro** Ⓣ 06 47021, Ⓦ www.bnl.it
- **Banco di Sicilia** Ⓣ 06 67141, Ⓦ www.bancodisicilia.it

ACCOUNT CHECKLIST

Bring the following with you when you apply to open an Italian bank account:

- ✓ Passport
- ✓ Your *permesso di soggiorno* (visitor's permit; see "Student Visas" in Chapter 1)
- ✓ Proof of residence
- ✓ Student ID card
- ✓ Cash for deposit

POSTAL SERVICES

The Italian postal system is reliable and affordable, although delivery speed tends to be on the slow side. Post offices, located all around the city, are usually open from 8:30 A.M. to 2:00 P.M. on weekdays and from 8:30 A.M. to 1:00 P.M. on Saturdays. (For details on locations and hours of specific branches, visit the Poste Italiane website at www.poste.it.) If a carrier attempts to deliver a package to your apartment when you're not home, you'll receive a notice telling you where you can pick it up.

A letter sent by *posta prioritaria* (regular mail) from Italy to the United States costs €1. An average package (up to 350 grams) costs about €7. Letters and packages sent overseas can take ten days or longer to be delivered; you can get faster delivery times by paying higher postage.

EXPRESS DELIVERY

If you need to get a package home fast, try one of the following overseas shipping services.

DHL Ⓣ 800 345 345 (pickup service only), Ⓦ www.dhl.it

Federal Express Ⓐ Via Barberini 115, Ⓣ 800 123 800, Ⓦ www.fedex.com, Ⓜ Barberini

Mailboxes, Etc. Various locations, Ⓦ www.mbe.com

APARTMENT LIVING

Living in an apartment on your own presents many pleasures—along with many responsibilities. On top of keeping the place reasonably clean, you'll have to set up and pay for utilities such as electricity, gas, garbage collection, and recycling. Italians rarely mail their payments, preferring to settle bills at the local post office, in person at each individual company, or with automatic deductions from their bank accounts. Here's a quick overview of the utilities, services, and other practicalities that are part of apartment living.

UTILITIES

- **Cable/Television:** Cable TV as Americans know it doesn't exist in Italy. If you want to watch more than the basic local stations, satellite TV is your only option. Getting the dish installed can be both difficult and expensive. You'll have to pay as much as €100 for the setup, and €30–€40 in monthly subscription fees. The following companies provide satellite service in Rome: Eurosat (www.lisspa. eu), Sat Elite Sky Digital Systems (www.satelite.it), and Suonimmagine (www.suonimmagine.it). Some smaller businesses offer lower prices and more personalized service as well. No one company has a monopoly, so shop around to find the best deal.

- **Electricity:** Electricity is very expensive in Italy. Sign up for service by calling ENEL (Ente Nazionale per l'Energia Elettrica) at 800 900 800 (prompts are in Italian) or go to the nearest office in person. Locations are listed on the company's website, www.enel.it.

- **Gas:** Most homes and apartments in Italy use gas for cooking and heating rather than electricity. Gas service is provided by ITALGAS (800 900 700, 800 987 898, 800 900 999, www.italgas.it) or VIVIGAS (800 151 313, www.vivigas.it).

- **Internet:** The most popular Internet service providers are Telecom Italia (www.telecomitalia.it), Vodafone Omnitel (www.vodafoneomnitel.it), and Wind (www.wind.it). These are also, not coincidentally, the top three wireless providers, so consider bundling your Internet and cell-phone plans for discounts on dial-up and/or toll-free local access numbers.

- **Telephone:** A landline is imperative if you want Internet service. Having a home phone is also a good idea if you'll be placing a lot of long-distance calls, as landline rates are more reasonable than cell phone rates (see "Calling Home" in Chapter 8). The largest and most popular service provider in Italy is Telecom Italia (www.telecomitalia.com). Initial setup costs about €200 and doesn't get you much except basic phone service, which runs around €15 a month. You will also be charged for all local and long-distance calls by the *scatto* (click), a unit of time that you can actually hear being counted while you're on the phone. To avoid the *scatto,* use a prepaid calling card.

SERVICES

- **Garbage:** Rome has strict garbage rules that are enforced by fines. You'll be responsible for disposing of your garbage by taking it to the closest garbage bin on the street, and you'll be required to do this on a certain day (pickup schedules vary by neighborhood). All garbage must be sealed in bags. Italy levies a heavy garbage collection tax on its residents, with the particular fees determined by the number of square meters a person rents or owns. Most landlords cover this fee for renters.

- **Locksmiths:** If you find yourself locked out of your apartment, be sure to have identification on hand: Locksmiths will let you in but they are required to stay until you present formal ID. A reliable locksmith in Rome is DF Serrature Porte, with twenty-four-hour service and English-speaking dispatchers. It can be reached toll-free at 800 774 764 or locally by calling 06 8632 2172, or online at www.dfserratureporte.it.

- **Maintenance:** If anything goes wrong in your apartment, call your landlord immediately. The landlord is responsible for all repairs and maintenance (unless you damage or break an appliance, in which case you'll have to get it fixed yourself). Do not call plumbers, electricians, or any other repair people on your own.

- **Recycling:** Unfortunately, recycling is not a widespread practice in Rome. If you live outside of university housing and want to recycle, you'll generally have to make your own arrangements with one of the handful of Rome's independent recycling companies. Pickup is once a month and will cost you about €30 each time. Check with your landlord or building manager to find out how to arrange service.

PRACTICALITIES

- **Converters and adaptors:** In Italy, as in most European countries, the standard outlet carries 220–240 volts (compared to 110–120 volts in the United States). Plugs are shaped differently as well. If you want to bring (and use) your favorite hair dryer or other electrical device from home, you'll need to buy a plug adaptor or a voltage adaptor/converter before you leave. Plug adaptors allow dual-voltage appliances (such as most laptops) to be plugged in, but they don't actually convert electricity. Voltage converters enable you to run small electrical appliances for short periods of time. Voltage transformers—sold in kits for about $30—let you use your larger appliances, such as CD players or TVs. Most Italian homes run on 3 kilowatts, meaning it's easy to blow fuses, so avoid using multiple appliances at one time.

- **Laundry and dry cleaning:** You'll find *lavanderie* (laundromats) and dry cleaners all around Rome, but they're perhaps not as ubiquitous as you'd like. The average self-service load will cost significantly more than it does in the United States: Expect to pay between €5 and €7 to wash and €7 and €10 to dry. For full wash-and-fold service, expect to pay up to €35 a load. Dry cleaning is also expensive: Expect to pay about three to four times what you would in the United States.

5 AFFORDABLE CITY ADVENTURES

1. **EUR:** Mussolini's famous Esposizione Universale di Roma (EUR) district, on the south end of the city, is full of monumental fascist architecture. Walk around and explore the buildings from the outside, or stop into the *Museo della Civiltà Romana* (Museum of Roman Civilization) to see a gigantic model of the ancient city. Ⓜ B—EUR Palasport, EUR Fermi

2. **Porta Portese:** Fighting your way through crowds, hunting for bargains, and warding off pickpockets make for an enjoyable Sunday morning in this Trastevere flea market. Ⓐ Via Portuense at Vi Nippolito Nievo, Bus Porta Portese

3. **Appian Way:** Picnic along *Via Appia Antica* (the ancient Roman road)—being careful not to wind up in the middle of a herd of sheep—and look for ancient bone fragments in one of the many underground catacombs. Bus San Sebastiano

4. **Villa Ada:** Discover this urban forest, near Parioli, that was once home to the royal Savoy family and today offers countryside activities in the heart of the city. You can rent a bike, a pony, or a canoe and pretend you're a nineteenth-century aristocrat whiling away the hours. Bus Via Salaria

5. **Self-designed walking tour:** Get out a map and track whatever interests you. Check out all the obelisks in town, for example, or hop from fountain to fountain. Have *a lot* of time on your hands? Set out to visit all of Rome's 900 churches!

7. Studying & Staying Informed

You'll find no shortage of quiet spots in Rome where you can hit the books while still feeling like you're close to the city's action. Around every corner, it seems, there's an amazing park where you can relax under an inviting tree—or, of course, a cafe where you can linger for hours. And if you drink enough espresso, you may even find that you can study all night.

If you're an information junkie, Rome won't disappoint. Newsstands around the city brim with local and international publications—including Italy's famous fashion magazines, which definitely fall on the lighter side of the journalistic spectrum. Italians read more books than Americans do, and they get their news primarily from newspapers (rather than from television or the Internet). The government controls a great deal of the media—and many Romans are cynical about this relationship—but in general, you will find that most Italian news sources are fair and balanced.

PLACES TO STUDY

Thanks to Rome's mild climate, you'll be able to take advantage of the city's natural beauty even when buckling down. When the weather does force you inside, there are a number of comfortable places to go. As you get to know the city, you'll find all sorts of nooks and crannies of your own. For starters, check these out.

The Alessandrina Library at La Sapienza University Hit the books with Italian students in this library's comfortable reading rooms. Ⓐ Piazzale Aldo Moro 5, Ⓣ 06 447 4021, Ⓦ www.alessandrina.librari.beniculturali.it, Ⓜ Policlinico

Bibli Café Browse the books, surf the web, and grab a light meal during study breaks at this inviting cafe in Trastevere.
Ⓐ Via dei Fienaroli 28, Ⓣ 06 581 4534, Tram Casteletto, Trastevere/Mastai

Biblioteca di Storia Moderna e Contemporanea (Library of Modern and Contemporary History) Past the amazing sixteenth-century courtyard, you'll find two comfortable rooms in which you can study or conduct research.
Ⓐ Via M. Caetani 32, Ⓣ 06 682 8171, Ⓦ www.bsmc.it/intro.php, Bus/Tram Largo Torre Argentina

Villa Borghese This vast and beautiful urban park has numerous wi-fi hotspots, so grab a blanket and a laptop and get to work. Reward yourself with a drink at the Casa del Cinema's open-air bar, also inside the park. Ⓐ Via Marcello Mastriani 1, Ⓦ www.casadelcinema.it, Ⓜ Spagna

Villa Mirafiori at La Sapienza University Explore the philosophy department's gardens and library for quiet places perfect for studying. Ⓐ Via Carlo Fea 2, Ⓣ 06 4991 7212, Ⓦ w3.uniroma1.it/filosofia, Ⓜ Piazza Bologna

LIBRARIES

If you're looking to get your work done at the neighborhood library, look again. Rome has dozens of municipal libraries throughout its neighborhoods, but in practice, few students use them. And while Rome also boasts world-class research libraries, they're intended for serious scholars and can be tricky to access. Your best bet is to stick with your university library for your study and research needs.

To join one of Rome's municipal libraries, you must present proof of your residence in Rome. Books are loaned for a month in most cases. Don't count on finding many English-language titles besides a few magazines and some popular novels. The largest branches lie outside of Rome's central district, but they can be accessed by public transportation. For more information, visit the government-run website for the city of Rome, www.comune.roma.it.

Municipio ROMA XI, Ostiense Ⓐ Via Ostiense 113 B, Bus Via Ostiense

Municipio ROMA XVI, Monteverde Nuevo Ⓐ Viale dei Colli Portuensi 275, Bus Porta Portese

ENGLISH-LANGUAGE BOOKSTORES

There are more than a dozen highly regarded English-language bookstores in Rome. In addition to reading materials in English, these bookstores also offer good places to network and find helpful services. Almost all have bulletin boards that allow free postings, so if you're looking for a roommate, someone to chat with in Italian, or even an English-speaking yoga teacher, these are great places to begin your search.

Almost Corner Bookshop Specializing in British literature, this cluttered, cozy Trastevere shop also has an excellent drama selection and dozens of local-interest books. Ⓐ Via del Moro 48, Ⓣ 06 583 6942, Bus Piazza Sonnino

Anglo American Bookstore You'll find this bookstore close to the high-end shops and the bedlam of tourists around the Spanish Steps. It specializes in British and American literature and has a good selection of books on art, architecture, and history. Science and technology books are housed at Via delle Vite 27, just down the street. Ⓐ Via della Vite 102, Ⓣ 06 679 5222, Ⓦ www.aab.it, Ⓜ Spagna

The English Bookshop The shelves in this small shop hold mostly British fiction, including a large selection of Victorian literature. You will also find stationery, cards, and translations of Italian literature. Ⓐ Via di Ripetta 248, Ⓣ 06 320 3301, Ⓜ Spagna

Feltrinelli International Feltrinelli is one of the largest bookstore chains in Rome. This branch offers a wide selection of foreign-language books, including books in English. Ⓐ Via Emmanuele Orlando 84, Ⓣ 06 482 7878, Ⓦ www.lafeltrinelli.it, Ⓜ Spagna

Lion Bookshop This small shop, not far from the Piazza del Popolo, is the oldest English-language bookstore in the city. It specializes in textbook orders but also has a fair selection of current British and American fiction. Ⓐ Via dei Greci 36, Ⓣ 06 3265 4007, Ⓜ Spagna

NEWSPAPERS

A typical Roman starts the morning at a local coffee shop with a newspaper grabbed at a tabacchi along the way. In fact, Romans make a bit of a ritual of discussing the news with friends and strangers, even the barista behind the counter. Italy is home to several major newspapers, each with a fairly obvious political leaning.

Corriere della Sera Rome's largest and most widely read newspaper (also considered the most politically moderate), with Italy's best coverage of international news. Ⓦ www.corriere.it

Il Giornale A more conservative choice. Ⓦ www.ilgiornale.it

Il Sole 24 Ore Italy's leading financial daily. Ⓦ www.ilsole24ore.com

La Repubblica A celebrity and entertainment tabloid that offers serious journalism as well; also the most liberal of the major papers. Ⓦ www.repubblica.it

La Stampa Based in Turin, with good coverage of the arts and humanities. Ⓦ www.lastampa.it

L'Unita Founded by communists but now rather moderate politically. Ⓦ www.unita.it

Roma C'è A popular listings paper, available at any newsstand. ⓦ www.romace.it

NEWSPAPERS IN ENGLISH

If you're aching for an English-language newspaper, your best bet is to check out the online version of your favorite paper from home. You can also try the *International Herald Tribune,* sold at any newsstand. For local news in English, check out "Italy Daily," an English-language insert in the *International Herald Tribune.* Other Roman English-language newspapers are less news-oriented but provide practical advice for English speakers living in Italy.

English Yellow Pages Technically a phone book for Italian businesses that cater to English-speaking residents, but features an ever-evolving website with information about housing, banking, and other practicalities. ⓦ www.intoitaly.it

The Informer An online publication for English-speaking foreigners in Italy, with an extensive and frequently updated section on Rome (€30 for a six-month subscription, €55 for one year) ⓦ www.informer.it

Wanted in Rome The oldest and most popular English-language newspaper, available at larger newsstands. ⓦ www.wantedinrome.com

MAGAZINES

The celebrity gossip and salaciousness (even nudity) to be found in Italian magazines makes American magazines like *Us Weekly* and *Star* seem tame by comparison. Italian fashion magazines, in particular, provide a clear window into the lascivious aspect of the Italian soul. In addition to hundreds of Italian choices, you'll find copies of *Newsweek, Time,* the

Economist, and other English-language titles readily available at newsstands. Here is a selection of popular Italian magazines.

Gente Viaggi A popular monthly magazine about exotic travel destinations around Italy and the world.
Ⓦ www.genteviaggi.it

L'espresso Italy's most popular weekly news-and-entertainment magazine, with gossip about musicians and film stars—including American celebrities.
Ⓦ espresso.repubblica.it

Max A general-interest monthly magazine for men, whose coverage includes photos of scantily clad women.
Ⓦ max.corriere.it

Viaggi e Sapori A monthly travel and food magazine.
Ⓦ www.quadratum.it

TV AND RADIO

Italy has three major television networks: *Raiuno, Raidue,* and *Raitre.* Run by the government, they resemble the major American networks. For additional viewing options, including English-speaking channels, try satellite television (see "Apartment Living" in Chapter 6 for information on how to hook it up). Here is a selection of popular Italian television and radio channels.

Canale 5 A private channel that offers mostly movies and entertainment programming. Ⓦ www.canale5.mediaset.it

Italia Uno and Rete 4 Two private channels focused on news, weather, and local and educational programming.
Ⓦ www.mediaset.it/italia1, Ⓦ www.mediaset.it/rete4

Le Sette and TeleMonteCarlo Two smaller stations that show a mix of old movies, reruns of syndicated shows, and the late-night game shows Italian TV is famous for (both included with basic television service).

Radio Centro Suono (101.3) Your best bet for easy listening, mostly Italian, but also some global new age. Ⓦ www.radiocentrosuono.it

Radio Citta Futura (97.7) Plays techno, punk, hard rock, and new wave. Ⓦ www.radiocittafutura.it

Radio Onda Rossa (87.9) Plays mostly alternative Italian and British music. Ⓦ www.ondarossa.info

Radio Radicale (91.5) Focuses on political programming, including left-wing news broadcasts. Ⓦ www.radioradicale.it

Radio Rock (106.6) Offers classic rock, both Italian and American Ⓦ www.radiorock.it

5 GOOD EXCUSES
NOT TO STUDY

1. **Evening passeggiatas:** You're not truly living as a Roman if you don't take an evening *passeggiata*, or a leisurely stroll before dinner. Put down your books and join the crowds wandering down the Via del Corso. Bus Via del Corso

2. **The Pantheon in the rain:** Visit the Pantheon during a rainstorm at least once. The drops hitting the ancient stone floors through the eye at the top of the dome truly is a sight to behold. (When it's sunny, the beams streaming through the hole are equally beautiful.) Pay your respects to the painter Raphael while you're there: His tomb is on the left-hand side. Bus/Tram Largo di Torre Argentina

3. **The pope:** Take a Wednesday morning off and join the official papal audience in St. Peter's Square. Ⓜ Ottaviano/San Pietro

4. **Soccer:** You need to attend at least *one* soccer match during your time in Rome. Books will be far from your mind when you take your place among the screaming fans.

5. **Hunger:** A freshly baked cornetto... A smooth, rich gelato that tastes even better as you stroll along the Tiber . . . A plate of warm pasta *alla carbonara* ... A hunk of crusty Italian bread ... Hunger is *always* a good excuse to ditch the books.

8. Staying in Touch

One of the most difficult aspects of moving to Rome is being separated from family and friends. While homesickness is a normal part of studying abroad, luckily there are loads of opportunities to stay connected—in real time—to those near and dear to you.

The Internet, with instant messaging and emailing, is the easiest and cheapest option. In fact, you'll probably find yourself on a first name basis with the proprietor of your neighborhood Internet cafe within a few weeks of your arrival. Cell phones are as ubiquitous in Rome as they are in most of the world. Many who land in the city (even for short stays) find that getting set up with an Italian mobile phone and service is essential to both feeling connected and mastering city life.

INTERNET

The easiest way to get online will probably be through your host school's computer lab. If you live in university housing, your dorm or apartment should be hooked up as well. When the computer labs are too crowded, you'll find that Internet cafes all over Rome offer a convenient alternative. (Or, if you have a laptop, keep alert for the wi-fi hotspots scattered around the city.) Internet cafes usually charge about €4 for an hour, in hourly or half-hourly increments. Try out a few different places until you find one with agreeable rates and atmosphere. Here's an Internet cafe that offers especially cheap rates.

EasyInternet Café Rates start at €0.50 per hour but vary depending on how many Internet users are in the cafe. Ⓐ Via Barberini 2, Ⓣ 06 4290 3388, Ⓜ Barberini

CELL PHONES

With rare exceptions, cell phones purchased in the United States won't work in Europe. If you want to use a cell phone during your stay in Rome, you'll almost certainly need to buy an Italian cell phone (about €50–€60) and investigate the area's various service plans.

USING RECHARGEABLE SIM CARDS

Pay-as-you-go SIM (subscriber identity module) cards are the best option if you'll be in Rome for a short time. With these prepaid microchips, you don't have to sign a contract with a cellular provider; you just slip the card (smaller than a postage stamp) into your phone and buy blocks of minutes as you need them. You can get minutes by purchasing *ricaricards*, which are pre-paid, password-protected cards that are rechargeable in denominations of €25–€100. Simply scratch off the card's secret code with a coin and follow the directions on the card for recharging your phone's minutes. *Ricaricards* are sold at cell-phone stores, tabacchi, and various other places around Rome. To use a SIM card, you'll need to purchase an Italian cell phone, except in te rare case that your U.S. phone is SIM compatible (see "Using Your U.S. Cell Phone").

SIGNING A CONTRACT

Signing up with an Italian provider is an option if you plan to stay in Rome for a long time—contracts normally require commitments of at least one year. Service plans are not as popular as ricaricards are, perhaps because providers don't give any kind of price break in exchange for loyalty. (Expect to be billed every two months.) Italy has three major service providers, all of which offer comparable rates. Do some serious comparison-shopping to find the best plan, and find out whether your university has arranged any special deals with a particular company. Here are your options.

- **Telecom Italia Mobile (TIM)** Ⓦ www.telecomitaliamobile.it
- **Vodafone Omnitel** Ⓦ www.vodafoneomnitel.it
- **Wind** Ⓦ www.wind.it

USING YOUR U.S. CELL PHONE

In certain cases, you may be able to use your current cell phone in Rome. If you have a multiband phone (check with your U.S. service provider to make sure), you can sign up for international roaming before you leave for Italy. But be forewarned: International roaming is very expensive and can result in astronomical phone bills. A more affordable option may be to switch your phone over to an Italian calling plan. Ask your U.S. service provider to unlock your phone so it will work on another provider's network, and double-check that the phone is compatible both with the Italian network you have chosen and with SIM-card technology.

CALLING HOME

Rest assured, there are several affordable ways to place international calls, and your friends and folks back home won't forget the sound of your voice. But remember: Rome is six hours ahead of the U.S. Atlantic coast—and nine hours ahead of the Pacific—so if you want to catch people at home and awake, you may have to stay up pretty late to make a call. If you have an Italian cell phone, all incoming calls are free, so do your best to convince your folks and friends back home to call you.

CALLING CARDS

Calling cards—which can be used from any cell phone, pay phone, or home phone—generally provide the best deals on international phone calls. Rates average between €0.10 and €0.20 a minute, but shop around. There are many types of calling cards in Italy, with prices depending on where you're calling and the type of phone you're calling from. You'll find the cards for sale at tabacchi, hotels, and supermarkets throughout the city.

To use an Italian calling card, you dial an access number, enter a password, and then dial the number of the phone you want to reach, including the country code. Two access numbers are on the card: The local number will give you more minutes, but you'll have to pay for the local call; the toll-free number will give you fewer minutes, but you'll save the cost of the local call. Calling cards typically expire within two months.

DIRECT CALLS

Calling direct is expensive. Long-distance calls from Italy to the United States average €0.40 a minute, whether you're calling from a landline or a cell phone. Landline rates for inter-European calls average €0.30 a minute.

PAY PHONES

You'll find pay phones on street corners all over Rome. Most accept not coins but *schede* (prepaid calling cards), which come in denominations of €5 and can be purchased at tabacchi. Slip your card into the slot on the pay phone, then dial the local or long-distance number you wish to call. When you are within 2 minutes of using up your allotted time, the phone will beep twice.

HOW TO DIAL INTERNATIONAL NUMBERS

Here's a quick guide to dialing international numbers from landlines. See the Appendix for a list of commonly used country codes.

Numbers in the United States Dial 00 + 1 + area code + number. For example, dial 001 555 123 4567.

Numbers in other countries Dial 00 + country code + city code + number. For example, to reach someone in Barcelona (city code 93), Spain (country code 34), you would dial 00 34 93 123 4567.

VOICE OVER INTERNET PROTOCOL

Voice over Internet Protocol, or VoIP, is the most economical choice for making international calls. With it, you place your calls with a computer and a high-speed Internet connection. The cheapest and easiest way to make VoIP calls is to use the computer-to-computer method, which is free if your friends and family have the same equipment you do. Calls to people who do not have VoIP equipment still cost very little—less than €0.05/minute for connections to the United States.

To set yourself up to use VoIP, you'll need a headset—or you can use the speakers and microphone that come integrated with most new laptops. If you don't have these items already, a trip to Media World in Rome (www.mediaworld.it) will get you what you need. Then, simply download the software from your chosen VoIP provider's website; it's probably best to stick to the big names, such as Vonage and Skype.

- **AIM (an America Online service)** ⓦ www.aim.com
- **Google Talk** ⓦ www.google.com/talk
- **Skype** ⓦ www.skype.com

- **Vonage** Ⓦ www.vonage.com
- **Yahoo** Ⓦ www.yahoo.com

5 THINGS ABOUT THE U.S. YOU WON'T EXPECT TO MISS—BUT WILL

1. **Jaywalking:** When in Rome, wait for the walk signal before you cross the street—or you take your life in your hands. Step into the street against the light, even if it looks clear, and suddenly a mass of speeding cars and Vespas will be heading right for you.

2. **Affordable jeans:** Shopping for clothes in the United States is bad enough, but wait until you realize that most jeans in Rome cost a small fortune. Even a pair of Levis can run €90, whereas designer jeans regularly go for €200 or more.

3. **English-language movies:** Although it's possible to find v.o. (original version) movies in Rome, international distributors tend to dub American movies into Italian rather than give them subtitles. You'll experience a strange disconnect when you hear a familiar Hollywood actor speaking Italian.

4. **Customer service:** Roman clerks are not known for their attentiveness—or even, sometimes, for their politeness. You'll be lucky to get a disdainful *ciao* in some stores. Different ideas about what good customer service entails may be one of the first things to spark culture shock.

5. **American-style breakfast:** Italians definitely don't regard breakfast as the most important meal of the day. Small pastries and smaller espressos, although delicious, may leave you pining for plates of scrambled eggs and sausage served with bottomless cups of coffee.

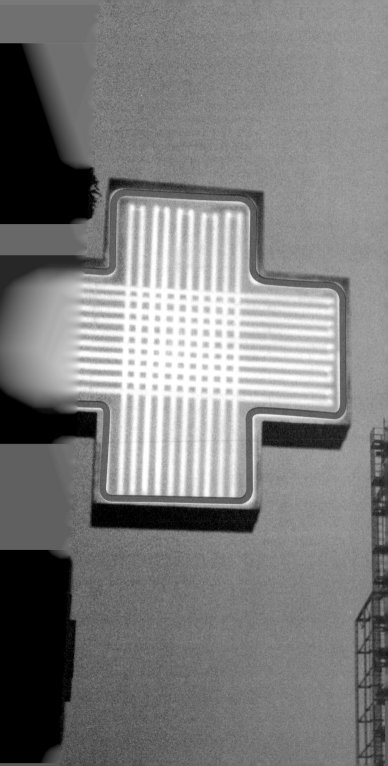

9. Health

Y**ou must have adequate** health insurance before you leave for Italy. You can't get a student visa without proof of insurance, and of course you'll want to be covered in case you get sick or injured. Your school will most likely work with you to make sure you have an appropriate policy for your time in Rome. But if, for whatever reason, your insurance situation is especially complicated, or if you think you may qualify to participate in Italy's state healthcare system, this chapter offers some quick information that may help.

Rest assured that the doctors in Rome are (in all likelihood) just as good as the doctors back home. Many of the Italian physicians who participate in American insurance plans are bilingual, so you should have no trouble finding an English-speaking doctor if you need one. Keep in mind, however, that the overwhelming majority of your medical encounters in Rome, such as discussions with the local pharmacist, will be conducted in Italian. For Italian words and phrases useful for visits to the doctor, pharmacy, or hospital, see "Useful Phrases" in the Appendix.

HEALTH INSURANCE

Most American insurance plans will reimburse you for your medical expenses, but they won't coordinate billing with European practices. In other words, you'll have to pay for all of your healthcare needs up front and out of pocket. This may sound daunting, but keep in mind that Italian fees for doctor visits, procedures, and medicines are just a fraction of what they are back home—cost shouldn't stop you from seeking medical attention if you need it.

Private health insurance plans vary in what they cover. Before leaving for Italy, verify with your provider exactly what your policy entitles you to and make sure you understand every detail, requirement, and exclusion. Come prepared with your insurance card and claim forms every time you visit a pharmacy, doctor, or hospital. Keep your receipts so that you can get reimbursed. Your insurance company may require detailed forms and receipts translated into English, with euros converted into dollars.

THE ITALIAN HEALTHCARE SYSTEM

The Italian healthcare system, run by the government body Unita Sanitaria Locale (USL), provides free health services to all Italian citizens. If you're eligible to receive benefits from the government, you pay no medical expenses out of pocket; you need only present your USL health card . Here are a few examples of who is and isn't eligible for Italian healthcare:

Who is eligible:

- Students enrolled directly in an Italian university (not through a study-abroad program)

- Anyone married to an Italian citizen

- Anyone who has a contract with a Italian employer

Who is *not* eligible:

- Students enrolled in an American study-abroad program

- Students enrolled to study Italian at a private language-instruction school

- Tourists

GETTING HEALTH COVERAGE IN ITALY

If you need to get health coverage after you arrive in Italy (and if you don't qualify for the free government system), here are a few insurance options:

- **USL:** It's possible to buy your way into the public healthcare system; you'll likely pay around €400 a year. To register, head to the USL office (Lungotevere Ripa 1, 06 59941, Vaticano metro stop), or check the Ministry of Health's website for more information (www.ministerosalute.it).

- **Private Italian insurance:** Many Italians opt to get private insurance despite their eligibility for free healthcare (waiting lists for medical appointments can be long, and public health facilities are not always as modern and sanitary as one might want). The cost of private Italian insurance varies, but is typically in the range of €1,000 a year. Members usually have to pay for services out of pocket, then file a claim. Options include Istituto Nazionale delle Assicurazioni (www.ania.it) and Filo Diretto (www.filodiretto.it).

- **Global medical insurance:** Global medical insurance offers you coverage at home and abroad; look for an insurer that offers individual policies.

- **Travel insurance:** Travel insurance policies typically include at least some level of medical and emergency coverage, and many even have policies that cover short-term residents of a foreign country. Most provide twenty-four-hour travel assistance and protection against trip cancellation, interruption, or delay, as well as coverage for lost or delayed baggage. Two reliable providers are Travel Guard International (www.travelguard.com) and Travel Insured International (www.travelinsured.com). You can compare these and a number of additional companies at www.insuremytrip.com.

PHARMACIES

In Rome, a pharmacy—not a doctor's office—should be your first stop if you're feeling under the weather. Pharmacists give impromptu medical consultations and suggest medications. You may be surprised at the number of ailments they can help you with.

Italian drugstores are instantly recognizable by the neon green crosses that hang above their entrances. If the cross is lit, the pharmacy is open for business. Typical hours are 9:00 A.M. to 7:00 P.M. (with frequent closings from 1:00 P.M. to 4:00 P.M.), but you won't be hard pressed to find a twenty-four-hour drugstore close by. At least one pharmacy in each neighborhood stays open all night on a rotating basis—and all are required to post the address of the nearest twenty-four-hour location. Most pharmacies have at least one English-speaking staff member, or at least someone accustomed to interpreting customers' best attempts at explaining symptoms in an unfamiliar language. Here are a few pharmacies that are especially popular with English speakers.

Farmacia Fabiana Ⓐ Via Appia Nuova 97, Ⓣ 06 7047 6298, Bus Via Cerveteri

Farmacia Internazionale Apotheke Ⓐ Piazza Barberini 49, Ⓣ 06 487 1185, Ⓜ Barberini

Farmacia Trinita dei Monti Ⓐ Piazza di Spagna 30, Ⓣ 06 679 0626, Ⓜ Spagna

Vatican Pharmacy Ⓐ Via di Porta Angelica (Cancello di Sant'Anna), Ⓣ 06 6989 0561, Ⓜ Vaticano

OVER-THE-COUNTER DRUGS

In Rome, over-the-counter drugs are kept behind the counter, so you'll have to speak with a pharmacist for all of your medication needs, however minor or embarrassing. For the most part, the same drugs sold without prescriptions in the United States are sold without prescriptions in Italy. If you have a run-of-the-mill headache, cold, flu, or upset stomach, you'll likely be able to get the medicine you need without any trouble. If you're not sure what you need or don't know the Italian equivalent of an American drug, describe your symptoms and ask for help. If you're looking for the Italian equivalent of a particular American drug, bring the empty bottle or package with you to show the pharmacist.

PRESCRIPTION DRUGS

In Italy, you can get your prescriptions from a pharmacist or a doctor, depending on your ailment. Antibiotics and sleep aids, for example, may be prescribed by a pharmacist, while birth-control pills require a doctor's prescription. You'll have to pay the full price for your medications up front, but prescription drugs in Italy are substantially less expensive than they are in the United States. Be sure to verify what type of prescription-drug coverage your American insurance provides, as well as what the claim procedures involve. Regardless of your insurance plan, Roman pharmacies will not file claims for you or log your insurance information into their computers—even if you have an Italian policy. You're responsible for filing any necessary insurance claims yourself.

VISITING THE DOCTOR

Fortunately, you'll have no problem finding an English-speaking physician, dentist, or mental-health professional in Rome. For comprehensive listings of health professionals in Rome, visit the U.S. Embassy's website at http://rome.usembassy.gov. Here's an overview of a few types of specialists you might see during your stay, as well as some advice on what to expect from your visits. (Before making any appointments, check with your insurance provider to confirm what's covered and to verify whom you're permitted to see.)

- **Physicians:** Italian attitudes toward doctors and medicine are a little different than you might be used to. Italians often don't go to the doctor when they are sick. Instead, they'll consult a pharmacist, or they may try to ignore the problem. At the same time, Italian doctors tend to have a fairly hands-off approach to healthcare. Know, too, that a medical office claiming to have English-speaking staff may not necessarily have an English-speaking doctor. Don't be surprised if a random staff member serves as a translator.

- **Dentists:** If Romans are reluctant to go to the doctor, they're doubly reluctant to go to the dentist. Dental care, especially preventive care, has just never been a priority. Most locals see a dentist only when they're in pain. Basic dental work also tends to be more expensive in Italy than it is in the United States. (Depending on your insurance, however, you may be partially or wholly reimbursed for the work you have done; check with your insurer.)

- **Optometrists/Ophthalmologists:** Private Italian insurance won't reimburse you for frames but may partially reimburse you for lenses—if you submit an ophthalmologist's written attestation that a new prescription is necessary. If you are eligible for USL services, basic eye care is covered in full.

- **Mental-health professionals:** English-speaking psychotherapists and social workers can help you with whatever issues you may face. Italian insurance doesn't typically cover psychological services, however, so be prepared to pay out of pocket.

- **Gynecologists:** Many gynecologists in Rome speak English, and their services are excellent in all categories, including preventive care, contraception, abortion, pregnancy, labor and delivery, and disease treatment.

HOSPITALS/EMERGENCY ROOMS

Rome has several full-service hospital facilities that cater to English-speaking clients. The ones listed below are among the best hospitals in Rome—even Pope John Paul II was often treated at the Rome American Hospital. (They are also private facilities, so consult your insurance provider for coverage specifics.) To locate other hospitals where English is spoken, visit the U.S. Embassy's website.

Calvary Hospital (Blue Nuns) Ⓐ Via S. Stefano Rotondo 6, Ⓣ 06 700 2441, Bus Via di Torrenova

Casa di Cura Assunzione di Maria Ⓐ Via Nomentana 311, Ⓣ 06 853 7231, Bus Nomentana

Rome American Hospital Ⓐ Via E. Longoni 69, Ⓣ 06 22551, Ⓦ www.rah.it, Bus Via Prenestina

Salvator Mundi International Hospital Ⓐ Viale delle Mura Gianicolensi 67, Ⓣ 06 58 8961, Bus Gianicolo

HELPLINES

If you find yourself suffering from problems such as anxiety, loneliness, homesickness, or substance abuse, don't hesitate to call either of the following hotlines, each of which has English-speaking staff.

Mario Mieli Cultural Association This nonprofit organization gives referrals for general crisis counseling as well as information on psychological and health issues specific to gays and lesbians. Ⓐ Via Efeso 5, Ⓣ 06 541 3985, Ⓦ www.mariomieli.it, Ⓜ San Paolo

Rome Samaritans Onlus This organization provides free crisis counseling for the full spectrum of mental-health issues. The Samaritans are not a religious group, despite their name. Ⓣ 800 860 022, Ⓦ www.samaritans-onlus.it

SEXUAL HEALTH ISSUES

Obtaining birth-control pills in Rome is relatively easy and inexpensive (usually under €10 a month). You'll just need to get a prescription first from an Italian gynecologist. Or, consider getting your American doctor to prescribe a six-month or a one-year supply of birth-control pills and fill the prescription all at once (if your insurance won't allow that, you can refill the prescription from Rome and have the monthly packets sent to you). The morning-after pill is also available from Italian pharmacies with a prescription. It must be taken within seventy-two hours following unprotected sex to be effective.

Abortion was legalized in Italy in 1978. Although many doctors will perform the procedure, some will not. Abortions are free to women covered by the

Italian healthcare system; all others must pay. For more information on abortions in Italy, go to BEN, the National Epidemiological Bulletin, at www.ben.iss.it/precedenti/aprile/1apr_en.htm.

SEXUAL HEALTH ORGANIZATIONS

Several organizations in Rome provide education about and assistance in women's health issues, such as contraception, disease prevention and gynecological care. One good option is the Associazione per l'Educazione Demografica (AIED). The Italian equivalent of Planned Parenthood, AIED provides low-cost care for women and men, regardless of residency status.

AIED Ⓐ Via Salaria 58, Ⓣ 06 884 0661,
Ⓦ www.aied.it, Ⓜ Spagna

5 IDEAS FOR CONQUERING HOMESICKNESS

1. **Gusto:** Dining at this Roman pizzeria/wine bar/restaurant that will make you feel like you're in the Big Apple instead of the Eternal City—as long as you ignore the ancient mausoleum of Emperor Augustus right outside. Ⓐ Piazza del Augusto Imperatore 9, Ⓣ 06 322 6273, Bus Piazza San Silvestro

2. **Abbey Theatre Pub:** Get your fill of Guinness *and* American sports at this satellite TV–equipped pub near Piazza Navona. Ⓐ Via del Governo Vecchio 51, 53, Ⓣ 06 686 1341, Ⓦ www.abbey-rome.com, Bus Chiesa Nuova

3. **McDonald's:** Enjoy an espresso courtesy of the golden arches. They're surprisingly decent and cost only €0.60. One sniff of that characteristic McDonald's aroma will transport you right back to the United States.

4. **Castroni:** Head to this grocery near the Vatican that sells Italian specialties *and* the treats you miss from home, like peanut butter and taco shells. Ⓐ Via Cola di Rienzo 196, Ⓣ 06 687 4383, Ⓜ Ottaviano/S. Pietro

5. **T-Bone Station:** Get your bar-food fix with chicken wings, onion rings, or nachos—not to mention tasty steaks and juicy hamburgers—at this American-style steak house. Ⓐ Via F. Crispi 29, Ⓣ 066786750, Ⓦ www.t-bone.it, Ⓜ Barberini

10. Getting Involved

Moving beyond your student horizons can take some effort. While your schoolwork will probably be your first priority, make the most of your time in Rome by getting involved in activities outside of school (schedule permitting, of course). You'll find endless opportunities to immerse yourself in Roman life, whether you're conducting scientific research through an internship, serving espresso at a cafe, or volunteering at a neighborhood hospital.

Getting to know Romans on a personal level takes some time, thanks to potential language barriers, intense family ties, and established friendships that began early in life. All the same, Romans are warm and welcoming when given enough time. Romans generally don't hold negative stereotypes about Americans—so it's up to you to make a good impression.

MEETING LOCALS

It may sound like a study-abroad cliché, but making an effort to befriend Romans should be a priority during your time abroad. Locals are excellent sources of practical and personal insights into the city, and the relationships you develop with them—whether the neighborhood newspaper vendor, the owner of the corner bar, or the chain-smoking guy in your art history class—will give you knowledge that would be impossible to gain from hanging out with Americans alone.

WHERE TO MEET ROMANS

Your university is the most obvious place to begin your pursuit of Roman friendships, whether you're lingering in the halls during breaks between classes, getting involved in extracurricular activities, or taking elective classes. Here are some ideas for making friends, both within and outside of school:

- Join an intramural sports team or participate in a sports club (see "Recreational Sports" in Chapter 13).

- Volunteer for a cause (see the "Volunteer Opportunities" section).

- Join a discussion group or a reading group at a neighborhood cafe—these are often advertised on university bulletin boards, at bookstores, and in English-language newspapers.

- Hang out in a bar—but remember that bars in Italy aren't like the ones you're used to in the United States. Although alcohol is served, the focus is less on drinking and more on coffee and conversation.

LANGUAGE EXCHANGES

If you want to make a new Roman friend and bone up on your Italian language skills at the same time, consider answering or posting an ad for a *scambio di lingua* (language exchange). During a language exchange, you and a native Italian speaker will meet for an hour or so, talking half the time in Italian and the other half in English. You can find and post ads on bulletin boards at your university, in language schools, or on websites such as rome.craigslist.org or www.wantedinrome.com.

DATING

The pace of dating in Rome is considerably slower than it is in the United States. Both men and women often prefer to go out with a group for a first, second, or even third date. Don't take it personally; young people in Rome just prefer a more communal dating scene. Roman men tend to be dominant, while women tend to let their dates take the lead. The way this plays out in daily life may seem sexist or it may seem gallant, depending on your perspective (if you're a woman, you may even find that you enjoy having doors held open for you). Here are a few tips for navigating the Roman dating scene:

- **Unwanted advances:** Italian men think nothing of approaching women at cafes, in bars, and even on public transportation. If you're a woman, your best weapon for fending off unwanted advances is to show you're not interested through your body language—Italian guys tend to pick up on even subtle cues.

- **Friendships:** Young Romans care a great deal about whether their friends like their dates. If you're into someone, make an effort to get to know his or her friends. At the same time, be aware that friendship is generally the default expectation in Rome's dating world: Expectations are usually very guarded on both sides.

- **Invitations:** Asking for a date is generally the province of men—it's uncommon for a woman to make the first move. Men are also usually expected to (and they expect to) pick up the tab for every expense, from transportation to dinner to drinks.

- **First dates:** Expect to go to a cafe for coffee or to a restaurant with a group of friends. Don't expect an American-style dinner for two followed by a movie.

CLUBS, ORGANIZATIONS, AND OTHER RESOURCES

Rome has an enormous international student community and an astonishing array of social groups, including several that connect American and other foreign students. Social groups are often informal and can be very local (often centered in particular neighborhoods). Look for groups that provide services or events that match your interests, and be sure to check with your university about student groups. You can locate promising groups on bulletin boards at universities, libraries, international bookstores, and language schools.

EXPAT RESOURCES

Social groups offer excellent opportunities to rub shoulders with other Americans. A number of bookstores, bars, and other places in Rome also draw an American crowd (for a list of English-language bookstores, see Chapter 7, "Studying & Staying Informed"; for bars and meeting places, see Chapter 16, "Night Life"). There's also a wide selection of expat resources that can provide advice on everything from finding housing to making new friends. You can start your investigation with these.

English Yellow Pages This site contains comprehensive listings of English-speaking services and facilities, along with a message board with postings advertising housing and jobs. A bimonthly newsletter serves as a clearinghouse for events around the city where you can meet other foreigners living in Rome. Ⓦ www.englishyellowpages.it

Expat Exchange Visit this site for an extensive message board, where you'll find listings for apartment rentals and job openings. Ⓦ expatexchange.com

Expats in Italy An excellent resource for recent transplants with advice on the practical aspects of moving to Rome. This group also holds monthly face-to-face meetings in various locations. Ⓦ www.expatsinitaly.com

Meetup This popular site gives international travelers a place to meet others with similar interests, swap travel experiences, and establish communities abroad. Ⓦ www.meetup.com

Transitions Abroad This is a good source of information for study-abroad students, long-term travelers, and expats. Ⓦ www.transitionsabroad.com

MEETING INTERNATIONAL STUDENTS

Rome is teeming with young Europeans, due in part to the fluid borders between E.U. nations and the popularity of Erasmus, a Europe-wide university exchange program. International youth congregate in various places throughout Rome, especially in student-heavy neighborhoods like Trastevere and San Lorenzo. Here are a few bars and cafes known for drawing students from all over the world.

Akab Cave This club, a Testaccio staple, attracts young people from throughout Europe with its dark, cavelike interior and its pulsing DJ tunes. Ⓐ Via di Monte Testaccio 69, Ⓣ 06 575 7494, Ⓜ Piramide

Café Latino This is the best place in the Rome to meet young South Americans—not least because of its live musical acts from Central and South America. Ⓐ Via di Monte Testaccio 96, Ⓣ 06 5728 8586, Ⓜ Piramide

Supperclub This trendy restaurant and club is perennially popular with young people from throughout Europe. Ⓐ Via de'Nari 14, Ⓣ 06 6880 7207, Bus Pantheon

Vineria An international crowd flocks to this wine bar and cafe because of its prime location on the Campo de' Fiori. Ⓐ Campo de' Fiori 15, Ⓣ 06 6880 3268, Bus Campo de' Fiori

VOLUNTEER OPPORTUNITIES

Rome offers endless opportunities to get involved in volunteer work—even if you only have one free afternoon each week, and even if your Italian isn't up to par. Serving meals at a homeless shelter, tutoring locals in English, and visiting patients in a hospital are just some of the possibilities. For ideas and details, ask what opportunities are available through your school, visit www.volontariato.com (a volunteerism portal), or check out one of the following organizations.

Greenpeace and the World Wildlife Federation (WWF) Both of these organizations have large constituencies in Rome. They offer wide-ranging volunteer opportunities. Ⓦ www.greenpeace.org, Ⓦ www.panda.org

Gruppi Archeologici d'Italia The Archaeological Groups of Italy is a nonprofit organization that sponsors volunteers for digs and preservation projects all over the country, including the Roman countryside. Ⓦ www.gruppiarcheologici.org

Slow Food This nonprofit is devoted to preserving Italy's culinary traditions. Many volunteer opportunities are available throughout the year. Ⓦ www.slowfood.it

U.S. Citizens for Peace and Justice This antiwar organization is devoted to education and activism, especially relating to the war in Iraq. They host a popular film series and often organize peaceful protests throughout Rome and other cities across the globe. Ⓦ www.peaceandjustice.it/volunteer.php

LGBT ORGANIZATIONS

In recent years, Italy's gay and lesbian community has become both more visible and more political. Although most of the political organizing happens in Milan, Rome is quietly becoming a cultural center for gays, lesbians, bisexuals, and transvestites—who for years kept almost completely underground. For listings of LGBT-friendly venues, see "Gay/Lesbian Bars and Clubs" in Chapter 16. Here are two popular organizations offering information and services for the LGBT community.

Arcigay This nationally prominent organization has an active branch in Rome and offers both counseling and information about LGBT-friendly establishments. Some gay bars and clubs require that patrons have an Arcigay membership card to enter. A one-year membership costs €14 and can be purchased at venues that require the card for admission. ⓣ 32 995 5453, ⓦ www.arcigayroma.it

Circolo Mario Mieli di Omosessuale Cultura The most visible gay and lesbian organization in Rome, this group also organizes Rome Pride, a gay-rights festival that takes place every July. ⓣ 06 541 3985, ⓦ www.mariomieli.org

5 FREE WAYS TO IMPRESS YOUR DATE

1. **Dine like the locals:** Take your date to a bar or restaurant where the proprietors know you so well that they shower you with affection when you walk in the door.

2. **Take a long walk in the Villa Pamphilj:** This amazing park in Monteverde Vecchio (near Trastevere) gets more impressive the deeper inside you go. Bus Ottovilla/Pamphilj

3. **Visit the Chiostro del Bramante:** Show off your cultural acumen by visiting these cloisters cum art exhibit hall at the Chiesa di Santa Maria della Pace. Ⓐ Vicolo del Arco della Pace 5, Ⓣ 06 686 1156, Ⓦ www.chiostrodelbramante.it, Bus Piazza Navona

4. **Climb every hill:** Choose your favorite of Rome's many hills and take in the romantic views at sunset. From Janiculum Hill, you can see the entire city laid out before you in a sea of rooftops and church domes (Bus Passeggiata del Gianicolo). And on Capitoline Hill, you can see the cityscape bisected by the Via del Corso from one side and the majestic Colosseum and Roman Forum from another. (Bus Piazza Venezia).

5. **See the lights:** Paris may be the city of lights, but Rome does its own share of nighttime glowing. A perfect way to start—or end—a romantic evening is to stroll past Rome's prettiest illuminated monuments: The Colosseum, the Pantheon, and Piazza Navona will all do nicely.

BUONGIORNO
GOOD MORNING

11. Working

Before you get too set on the idea of working during your time abroad, talk to an advisor in your study-abroad office to learn more about what you're in for. On the one hand, working brings more money—not an unwelcome thing, given the unfavorable exchange rate. It also presents a unique opportunity to get to know Italian culture up close and personal.

However, working also means facing a time-consuming job search and a visa-application process so convoluted it will leave your head spinning. And if you do take on a job, the time you spend bartending or tutoring takes away from time for studying, traveling, bar-hopping, museum-going, and doing all the other cool activities that brought you to Rome in the first place.

JOB HUNTING

Here are some quick tips for finding work in Rome:

- **Newspapers:** You'll find extensive help-wanted sections in newspapers, such as *Corriere della Sera,* which is also available online at www.corriere.it/lavoro.

- **Websites:** Peruse the English-language resources on Craigslist Rome (http://rome.craigslist.org), the English Yellow Pages (www.englishyellowpages.it), and Expat Exchange (http://expatexchange.com). You can also find job listings on websites such as www.jobpilot.it (the largest such database in Rome), www.assioma.org, www.cambiolavoro.com, and www.easyjob.it, all of them written in Italian only.

- **Networking:** As is the case for most job searches, networking will probably be your most effective tool. A good place to start is your home university, which may have an alumni organization in Rome. For other networking opportunities, see the "Expat Resources" section in Chapter 10.

TYPES OF JOBS

You already have a major asset that will come to your aid if you take up a job search: your fluency in English. Your native language makes you eminently qualified for several jobs, including teaching English, taking care of children, and working in cafes and restaurants (especially anglophone establishments). Of course, this being Rome, the vast majority of employers will require that you speak adequate Italian as well.

INTERNSHIPS

More and more, students are incorporating internships into their time abroad—either during the semester or over the summer after classes end. Many students are able to balance work and school, and an internship can provide an excellent opportunity to explore a possible career path or to gain extra experience during your time abroad. Your university's study-abroad office is your best resource for learning more. The following websites also offer general information on overseas internships.

- **Global Experiences** Ⓦ www.globalexperiences.com/internships
- **Institute for the International Education of Students** Ⓦ www.iesabroad.org
- **Intern Abroad** Ⓦ www.internabroad.com
- **International Internships** Ⓦ www.international-internships.com
- **Transitions Abroad** Ⓦ www.transitionsabroad.com/listings/work/internships/index.shtml

WORKING UNDER THE TABLE

Many young people from abroad engage in under-the-table work during their time in Italy, taking on undocumented jobs such as working in a cafe or bar run by a willing owner. Though such options are popular, this kind of work setup is illegal for both employee and employer. Even if the chances of being caught are slim, know that you're taking a risk if you go this route.

TEACHING ENGLISH

Teaching English is among the most in-demand occupations for young Americans living in Rome. The pay is typically low, but the work is rewarding—and the experience gives a boost to your résumé. Here are a few options worth considering.

- **Language schools:** Rome has a number of private schools that specialize in teaching English to adults, typically businesspeople. Most programs are designed for Italians, but you'll likely work with students of many different native languages. Every school has different requirements and the pay varies widely. The better programs offer €25–€30 an hour. Language schools to check out include Ambrit International School (www.ambrit-rome.com), American Overseas School of Rome (www.aosr.org), and The New School (www.newschoolrome.com).

- **Italian universities:** Universities sometimes hire Americans to teach courses in English grammar or literature, or to assist professors with duties such as grading papers and quizzes. You'll likely need a graduate degree, or at least some teaching experience, to pursue this sort of work.

TEFL COURSES

Programs in Teaching English as a Foreign Language (TEFL) provide lesson plans, teaching practice, and assistance in finding overseas teaching jobs. The monthlong courses can be expensive—most cost around $2,000. Enrolling in one can't hurt, but keep in mind that many Roman employers are simply looking for native-English-speaking teachers and couldn't care less about certification. Two of the most reputable TEFL courses are the Cambridge Certificate in English Language Teaching to Adults (www.cambridgeesol.org) and the Trinity Certificate in Teaching English to Speakers of Other Languages (www.trinitycollege.co.uk). For more information and a full list of courses, check out www.tefl.com.

TUTORING

Private tutoring can be an excellent option if you have a flexible schedule. You can fix your own rates, so you may be able to earn more money than you would at a language school. And tutoring is off the books, so you won't need a work visa. To find tutoring jobs, post fliers advertising your English skills at universities, bookstores, and other places frequented by people interested in learning languages. You can also post ads for free on the English Yellow Pages website, www.englishyellowpages.it. As a safety precaution, be sure to meet your students in a public place.

AU PAIR WORK

Among young Americans living in Italy, working as an au pair is second in popularity to teaching English. As a live-in babysitter, you might be asked to mind the children, tutor them in various subjects (including English), and perform light household chores; the details should always be negotiated prior to accepting a position. Often, au pair jobs will include fringe benefits like free travel with your host family. The downside tends to come in the form of curfews, house rules, and restrictions on what you can do during your time off.

Pay is based on the number of children in the household. Although your salary will be more of a stipend than an income, you'll get free housing in almost all cases. Commitments of more than a year are rare; short-term contracts for a summer or a semester are common. Here are some highly regarded au pair agencies to check out.

- **Agenzia Intermediate** Ⓣ 06 574 7444, Ⓦ www.intermediateonline.com
- **Angels Staff Services Association** Ⓣ 06 678 2877, Ⓦ web.tiscali.it/angelsstaff
- **Baby Bear Household Services** Ⓣ 06 5228 3342, Ⓦ www.babybear.it

GETTING PAPERWORK IN ORDER

The primary obstacle to working in Italy is getting legal permission to do so. Work visas, which are granted by the Italian government and required for aboveboard jobs, are not easy to come by. As a student visa holder, you're theoretically entitled to work up to twenty hours per week, but the student visa itself won't suffice as a work permit. Before you may work, you must first receive a job offer from an Italian employer—then apply to the Italian Labor Ministry for a *permesso di soggiorno per lavoro* (work card). Once you've been officially hired, you must obtain a *coda fiscale,* or tax ID number, before you can be paid legally.

5 SMALL LUXURIES TO REQUEST FROM HOME

1. **Peanut butter:** Sure, you'll find peanut butter for sale in Rome, but it's just not the same. The consistency is grittier, the taste less sweet.

2. **Beauty products:** If you're partial to a particular brand of hair gel or moisturizer, bring it with you—or have your folks send it. American beauty products sold in Roman salons or department stores can cost double what you'd pay at home.

3. **Cold and headache medicines:** For whatever reason, the Italian versions of cold and headache remedies just don't seem to work as well as American brands like Advil, Tylenol, and Robitussin. They're also sold in much smaller quantities per bottle.

4. **English-language books or magazines:** Even at Rome's international bookshops and newsstands, the selection of new fiction and magazines in English is limited—and the price is high. An American *Vogue,* for example, may cost about €8; a paperback novel will set you back €15 or more.

5. **Tea:** Italy is a coffee-drinking country. If you prefer tea, you'll be disappointed by the limited selection and quality, even in the big supermarkets.

12. Fitness & Beauty

Rome's fitness culture is a slowly evolving animal. The vast majority of Romans of all ages get their exercise by walking the city's streets and climbing its tree-lined hills. That said, most gyms offer fitness classes as well as instruction in organized sports, and many young people are taking up yoga and Pilates. Running and jogging haven't really caught on among Romans, who prefer walking leisurely—you can witness this firsthand during the evening *passeggiata* (stroll). Rome is, nonetheless, a wonderful city for running, as long as you stick to marked trails away from traffic and smog.

Rome's high-end salons and beauty shops will, sadly, be out of a student's budget. Hotel spas are generally intended for guests, although some luxury hotels are beginning to market their services to locals at reduced rates. Old-fashioned beauty parlors and barbershops are the first choice among Romans for basic services such as haircuts, manicures, pedicures, and facials.

GYMS AND SPORTS CLUBS

The best place to get your gym time in is at school, where exercise facilities (if they exist) are generally available for free or for a minimal fee. Gyms and sports clubs in Rome are on the expensive side and tend to be fairly small, with limited equipment. The fitness centers listed here offer the usual mix of cardio machines, free weights, and group classes. Rates vary depending on the gym and the services you choose; in general, a one-day pass ranges from €7 to €15, a monthly pass from €30 to €75. Be sure to inquire about student discounts.

Farnese Fitness Ⓐ Vicolo Delle Grotte, 32, Ⓣ 06 687 6931,
Ⓦ www.farnesefitness.com, Bus Campo de' Fiori

Fitness Express DLFOSTER Ⓐ Via dei Coronari 46,
Ⓣ 06 686 5248, Ⓜ Cipro–Musei Vaticani

Fleming Fitness Ⓐ Via Flaminia Vecchia 611,
Ⓣ 06 334 0535, Bus Via Flaminia Vecchia

Roman Sport Center Ⓐ Via del Galappatoio 33,
Ⓣ 06 321 8096, Ⓦ www.romansportcenter.com, Ⓜ Spagna

S.G. Roma Ⓐ Via del Muro Torto 5, Ⓣ 06 488 5566, Ⓜ Spagna

SWIMMING POOLS

Rome's public swimming pools are mostly the territory of school kids on humid summer afternoons. Swimming isn't popular in general, even during the hot summer months. Options for serious swimmers include purchasing a local membership at a hotel (see the "Spas" section for details) or investigating pool availability at area fitness centers (see the "Gyms and Sports Clubs" section). Entrance fees for other pools start at about €3 and can go as high as €15; in general, membership is not required. Here are a few swimming options.

Accademia del Nuoto For serious swimmers only.
Ⓐ Via Poggio Ameno 63, Ⓣ 06 594 0169, Bus Via Cristoforo Colombo

Centro Sportivo Cassia Nuoto Ⓐ Via Acqua Traversa 251,
Ⓣ 06 331 2732, Bus Via Cassia

Romano Sistemi Automatizzati Ⓐ Via Modena 32,
Ⓣ 06 481 8451, Bus Via Nazionale

RUNNING ROUTES

Rome is about as scenic a city as you're likely to find, and it's easy to find a running path that will take you through centuries of historic sites. There's even a tour company, albeit an expensive one, that specializes in historic jogging tours (see www.sitejogging.it for details). The safest way to do your miles is to find a marked trail away from the hustle and bustle of Vespas and cars (and the pollution they spit out)—the city's many parks are your best bet. Trails are typically open from sunrise to sunset, even if the park's other areas have more limited hours. Here are a few areas to check out.

Circus Maximus Ancient Rome's site for chariot races and staged naval battles is now a popular place for jogs. You'll feel centuries of history under your feet. Ⓜ Circo Massimo

Pincio Hill High above the Spanish Steps, just around the corner from Piazza del Popolo, and bordering the Villa Borghese, the Pincio is one of Rome's most beautiful places to jog. It features 11 miles of scenic, mostly wooded trails. Ⓜ Flaminio, Spagna

Villa Ada Located in the northern part of the city, Villa Ada is a large park that offers comprehensive trails for all abilities. Bus Via Salaria

Villa Doria Pamphilj Near the city center, this private park (and museum) offers a fee-accessed jogging trail. Lockers and showers are provided. Bus Via di San Pancrazio

YOGA AND PILATES

Aficionados will be happy to know that both yoga and Pilates have been embraced by Italians. Many hotel gyms and spas offer classes at reasonable rates (non–hotel guests are welcome). Classes range from €10 to €15, but many places offer a discounted price of about €7 for students. Investigate fitness centers (see the "Gyms and Sports Clubs" section) for options. Here are few additional places that offer a wide range of yoga or Pilates classes.

Amrita Centro Yoga e Ayurveda
Ⓐ Via Cristoforo Colombo 436, Ⓣ 06 541 3504, Ⓜ Marconi

Centro Yoga Vedanta Sivananda Ⓐ Via Oreste Tommasini 7, Ⓣ 06 4549 6529, Ⓦ www.sivananda.org/rome/index_files/Page325.htm, Ⓜ Bologna

Moves Fitness Center Ⓐ Via dei Coronari 6, Ⓣ 06 686 4989, Ⓦ www.moves-fitness.com, Ⓜ Cipro–Musei Vaticani

Pilates Roma (four locations) Ⓦ www.pilates-roma.com

Serafino Ambrosio (Il Metodo Pilates e Gyrotonic)
Ⓐ Via delle Milizie 40, Ⓣ 06 372 2303, Ⓦ www.ilmetodo.it, Bus Viale Giulio Cesare

HAIR SALONS AND BARBERSHOPS

The old-fashioned beauty parlor is still a venerable institution in Rome. Visiting a small neighborhood place is also a good way to save a few euros—as long as you don't mind having your hair cut or styled by a grandmotherly or grandfatherly type. A haircut at a salon such as Aveda (see the "Spas" section) can cost upwards of €40; a basic trim at a neighborhood shop runs about €25. All of the salons and beauty parlors listed here cater to both men and women and have at least some English-speaking staff.

Bruno e Massimo Necci Ⓐ Via Frattina 38, Ⓣ 06 679 4516, Ⓜ Spagna

Fabrizio Ⓐ Via Nomentana 251A, Ⓣ 06 440 2269, Ⓦ www.revolutionteam.it, Ⓜ Piramide

Ripetta 9 Ⓐ Via di Ripetta 9, Ⓣ 06 361 0390, Ⓜ Spagna

Walter Ⓐ Via G.G. Porro 16, Ⓣ 06 808 4695, Bus Piazza delle Muse

SPAS

A visit to a spa in Rome won't come cheap—the trip can cost €50 or more. Spas are not just for women: Roman men also enjoy getting massages and facials, even pedicures. Most of the city's best spas are found in hotels, but day spas are popping up in the trendier and more expensive neighborhoods. If indulgence is what you're looking for, investigate these options.

Aveda Day Spa Expect to pay a lot here. Offerings include facials (starting at €50), massages (starting at €85 for 60 minutes), haircuts start at €40, and various stress-relief and rejuvenation treatments. Ⓐ Rampa Mignanelli 9, Ⓣ 06 6992 4257, Ⓦ www.avedaroma.com, Ⓜ Spagna

Cavalieri Hilton This excellent hotel facility has a swimming pool and offers à la carte spa services that include massages, facials, waxes, manicures, pedicures, and mud wraps. Ⓐ Via Cadlolo 101, Ⓣ 06 3509 2241, Ⓦ www.cavalieri-hilton.it, Bus Via Cadlolo

Hotel de Russie Services here are priced à la carte and include facials, massages, manicures, pedicures, and wraps for hands and feet. Ⓐ Via del Babuino 9, Ⓣ 06 32 8881, Ⓦ www.hotelderussie.it, Ⓜ Flaminio

Terme di Fiuggi If you have the time, it's worth the effort to take a day trip outside the city to this thermal bath, which offers the ultimate in relaxation. Single-entry tickets during the high season (June to October) start at €5.50; during the low season (November to May), they start at €3.50. Ⓣ 07 75 5451, Ⓦ www.termefiuggi.it, Ⓣ Anagni-Fiuggi

5 CHEAP, TOURISTY THINGS YOU'VE *GOT* TO DO

1. **The Colosseum:** Stand inside the Colosseum and imagine the thousands of gladiators, animals, and Christian martyrs who were sacrificed right before the eyes of ancient Roman citizens. Admission is €12.50. Ⓜ Colosseo

2. **The Piazza del Campidoglio:** Visit Michelangelo's magnificent and serene architectural masterpiece. You'll find it in Piazza Venezia, at the top of the giant staircase. While you're there, check out the surrounding Capitoline Museums (admission is €6.50). Ⓣ 06 8205 9127, Ⓦ www.museicapitolini.org, Ⓜ Colosseo

3. **A boat ride on the Tiber:** Get a fish-eye view of Rome, gliding past stunning churches, impressive bridges, and historic Tiber Island. Several tour companies operate near Castel Sant'Angelo, with prices ranging from €9 (for a morning sightseeing cruise) to €30 or more (for dinner or evening wine cruises).

4. **Cemeteries:** Indulge your morbid side at the Chiesa di Santa Maria della Concezione's Capuchin cemetery, where the bones of more than 4,000 monks are artfully displayed in the walls themselves. Ⓐ Via Veneto 27, Ⓣ 06 487 1185, Ⓜ Barberini

5. **The Galleria Borghese:** See works by Bernini, Caravaggio, and Raphael, among other Italian greats. Admission is €8.50. Ⓐ Piazzale del Museo Borghese, Ⓣ 06 32 8101, Ⓦ www.galleria-borghese.it, Ⓜ Spagna

12. FITNESS & BEAUTY

13. Sports

Whether you're stiff from studying or worn out from museum-hopping, you'll find that Rome offers plenty of physical activities to get your blood pumping. Solo pastimes like hiking and cycling are more popular than team sports—except, of course, for the local soccer leagues—and you'll find plenty of good trails in and around the city.

While in Rome, you'll have to transfer your passions for American sports to *calcio* (soccer). There's no better place in Italy to see a soccer match than Rome's *Stadio Olimpico* (Olympic Stadium), home to two world-class soccer clubs. Whether you go to a match or watch in a bar with a crowd of locals, you'll find that no twist or turn of the game is too small to generate a boisterous reaction.

RECREATIONAL SPORTS

Italians are more likely to pursue culinary adventures than athletic ones, but you'll still find plenty of outdoor activities to choose from. Hiking is accessible to everyday athletes and advanced climbers both, depending on what trails you pick. And the popularity of cycling—always a favorite Italian spectator sport—has inspired many Romans to give up their Vespas for bikes: Join them, and you'll discover a great way to see the city and get some exercise at the same time.

HIKING

Several unofficial hiking trails lead up Rome's famous hills, rewarding climbers with panoramic views of the city. If you want a really good nature hike, however, you'll need to head out of the city. Try the Lepini Mountains to the south, the Monterano Natural Preserve to the north, or Lago di Bolsena to the northwest; all are less than two hours from central Rome.

Lepini Mountains Bring a map or a knowledgeable friend, as the trail markings are not particularly thorough. The best way to get there is to take a local (slow) train from Stazione Termini to Latina Station, then transfer to a bus headed for Norma, a little town at the foot of the mountains (there are no bus numbers, so confirm the destination before you board). If you want to drive, take the Appian Way (Via Appia Antica) south out of Rome; exit at Cisterna di Latina and follow the signs to Norma. Once in Norma, you can hire a guide or rent a bike. The trailhead is just off the main square.

Monterano Nature Reserve A Roman hiking experience if there ever was one, you'll see an abundance of wildlife *and* a smattering of Etruscan tombs along the marked trail. The location is fairly remote, so it's best to go by car. Take Via Aurelia north to the A12 highway. Exit at Cerveteri-Ladispoli, follow the signs to Bracciano, then take a left toward Canale Monterano, where you'll see signs for the reserve. If you want to go by public transportation, take a local train from Stazione Termini to Cerveteri, then a bus to Bracciano. Ⓦ www. monteranoriserva.it

---

Lago di Bolsena The area surrounding this enormous volcanic lake provides plenty of trekking opportunities. To reach the trails by public transportation, take the local train to Viterbo and transfer to any bus marked Bolsena. By car, take the A1 highway to the Orvieto exit, head toward Viterbo, then follow the signs to Bolsena. Ⓦ www.lagodibolsena.org

---

CYCLING

Serious cyclists should visit the English-language website of the *Federazione Italiana Amici della Bicicletta* (Italian Federation of Urban Cyclists and Bicycle Tourism), www.fiab-onlus.it. Here, you'll find maps of long-distance bike routes throughout Italy, as well as information about group cycling events in and around Rome. (See "Bikes" in Chapter 3 for tips on renting or buying a bike in Rome.) Here are a few additional cycling options.

Tiber River path A favorite of local cyclists, this path begins near the Vatican, meanders north to the stadiums of Foro Italico, then runs along 4 miles of the Tiber River. Ⓜ Ottaviano/San Pietro

Villa Borghese This mammoth park has plenty of traffic-free paths, though you'll have to share space with walkers, runners, and rollerbladers. Ⓜ Flaminio

CAMPING

The number of campsites in and around Rome is surprisingly high. Be sure to inquire at each campsite about rules, restrictions, and safety tips. The prices listed below apply during the low season; in high season (generally April, July, and August), expect to pay about €1 more per person and per tent.

Flaminio Village Bungalow Park This park offers airport transfer service, private campsites, and dorm-style accommodations (for those who don't want to sleep under the stars). Rates: €9.50 per person, plus €5.30 per tent. Ⓐ Via Flaminia Nuova 821, Ⓣ 06 333 2604, Ⓦ www.villageflaminio.com, Tram #2 to Piazza Mancini, then Bus #200 to the campsite, or Ⓣ Roma-Nord to Due Ponti

Seven Hills Village This camping destination lies just outside the city walls, about 15 minutes from the city center by metro. A pool, clean showers, and restrooms are available on site. Rates: €8.50 per person, plus €5 per tent. Ⓐ Via Cassia 1216, Ⓣ 06 3031 0826, Ⓦ www.sevenhills.it, Ⓜ Valle Aurelia to line FM3 to La Giustiniana

Tiber Hostel and Camping Only 20 minutes from downtown Rome by bus, this campsite offers tent platforms, cabins, free Internet access, and inexpensive airport transfers. Rates: €9.50 per person, plus €5.10 per tent. Ⓐ Via Tiberina, Ⓣ 06 3361 2314, Ⓦ www.campingtiber.com, Ⓣ Roma-Nord to Prima Porta, then shuttle bus to the campsite

OTHER SPORTS

If you're looking for other ways to get in on the action, bulletin boards at your university, in bookstores, and in cafes are great places to start your search. You can also check out the listings on websites such as www.wantedinrome.com and http://rome.craigslist.org. Here are just a few of the many options available.

Horseback riding For horses and trails within the city limits, visit the Galoppatoio in the Villa Borghese (Ⓐ Viale del Galoppatoio 23, Ⓣ 06 322 6797, Ⓜ Flaminio, Spagna). Further out, try Macchia Grande Farm in Trevignano Romano, about 45 kilometers away (Ⓣ 334 861 4801, Ⓦ www.trevignanoromano.it, see website for travel directions).

Soccer To find a local soccer club, visit the nearest city park and check the *ufficio di sport* (sports office) for information on what's available. Clubs play at all levels.

Rock climbing Some of Italy's best rock climbing can be found at Gran Sasso (literally, the big stone) in Abruzzo, 75 minutes outside the city. To go by public transportation, take a local train from Stazione Termini toward Fara Sabina to Stazione Tiburtina, then take a bus to L'Aquila. To go by car, take the A24 highway, exit at Assergi, and follow the signs to Campo Imperatore. Ⓦ www.gransassolagapark.it

SPECTATOR SPORTS

To most Italians, soccer is the only spectator sport that really matters, although other athletic competitions do get some attention from time to time. Do not leave Rome without attending at least one soccer match. The fans' exuberance, along with the sheer energy in the stadium, will make for an unforgettable experience. Another great way to experience this quintessential slice of Italian culture is to head down to a local bar and watch a match on TV with your neighbors.

SOCCER

Rome's two top-rated soccer teams, AS Roma and SS Lazio, share the *Stadio Olimpico* (Olympic Stadium). You can purchase tickets directly from the stadium box office or get them through merchandising outlets online. Don't expect any student or youth discounts. Because the stadium is so large, however, regular-season matches don't always sell out. If you show up in person you just might be able to score same-day tickets, which are deeply discounted on the rare occasions they're available.

Stadio Olimpico Ⓐ Viale del Foro Italico, Bus Foro Italico

ROME CITY MARATHON

The annual Rome City Marathon, held in early spring, attracts more and more spectators every year. Starting at the Colosseum, the race passes through some of Rome's most beautiful public squares, including Pizza Navona and the Spanish Steps. For more information or a complete route map, visit the official website, www.maratonadiroma.it.

TENNIS

Every May, Rome hosts the Italian Open, one of the most important European tennis tournaments outside the four Grand Slams. The tournament is held at the Foro Italico (a sports complex that includes the Stadio Olimpico), in the northern end of the city. For tickets and information, try www.tennistickets.com or the official tournament site, www.internazionalibnlditalia.it.

Foro Italico Ⓐ Viale del Foro Italico, Bus Foro Italico

5 MORE REASONS TO LOVE ROME (AS IF YOU NEEDED MORE REASONS . . .)

1. **History lessons:** In Rome, new pieces of the city's ancient past are discovered all the time. Two new metro lines are being constructed in the historic center, for example, and the diggers frequently run into previously unknown ancient ruins—forcing them to work around what they find.

2. **Autumn in the city:** The October sunlight splashing against palazzo walls is nothing short of stunning, and cobblestones glistening in the November rain exude a romance all their own.

3. **Discovering new neighborhoods:** Even if you live in Rome for years, you'll never run out of places to discover. For instance, check out the EUR (the Esposizione Universale di Roma), a southern district completely overlooked by most tourists: It showcases the impressive modernist architecture of fascist Rome. Ⓜ EUR Palasport, EUR Fermi

4. **Parco della Musica:** When you're ready for a study break, take in the amazing selection of music and theater at Renzo Piano's 2002 auditorium, a huge space with three concert halls, several smaller studios, and an open-air amphitheatre. Ⓐ Via P. de Coubertin 15, ⓣ 199 109 783, Ⓦ www.auditorium.com, Bus Auditorium (Bus M runs specifically for auditorium events)

5. **Teatro Valle:** Although it's less famous than the Teatro Argentina or the Teatro Dell'Opera di Roma, Teatro Valle is a must-see. You can take in the best classic and new works of the Italian stage, or catch one of the theater's occasional English-language productions. Ⓐ Via del Teatro Valle 23a, ⓣ 06 6880 3794, Ⓦ www.teatrovalle.it, Bus Largo Torre Argentina

14. Cultural Activities

You'll feel awed, to say the least, living and studying a stone's throw away from countless artistic treasures. Rome is perhaps best known for its ancient architecture, which you can see throughout the city without even making an effort just by strolling along the streets. Italy also boasts a long history of excellence in filmmaking, and Italian cinema, both past and present, is among the most politically charged in the world.

But art, architecture, and film are just three cultural strengths among many. Romans of all ages like to go out on the town and immerse themselves in the city's cosmopolitan riches. Many unique Italian festivals and traditions add even more excitement to an already overloaded city. In other words, you would have to work hard to be bored in Rome.

MUSEUMS AND GALLERIES

Rome houses particularly excellent collections of antiquities (both Roman and Egyptian) and Renaissance painting and sculpture. Because the city is home to the Vatican, it's also the best place to get acquainted with Catholicism's long artistic history. Discounted student tickets are offered by most museums, although some restrict the discounts to E.U. citizens (be sure to ask). Many museums are closed on Mondays. Here are some must-sees.

Capitoline Museums Second only to the Vatican Museums in size and popularity, this impressive collection features fascinating busts of Roman emperors as well as several Bernini sculptures. Highlights include Caravaggio's painting *The Fortune-Teller,* the ancient statue *Dying Gaul,* and the Etruscan statue *Capitoline Wolf,* which depicts a wolf nursing Romulus and Remus (who, according to mythology, founded Rome) and is now a city symbol. **Admission:** regular €6.50; reduced €4.50. **Hours:** 9 A.M. to 8 P.M. Tuesday through

Sunday; 9 A.M. to 2 P.M. on December 24 and 31; closed
Mondays, January 1, May 1, and December 25. Ⓐ Piazza del
Campidoglio 1, Ⓣ 06 3996 7800, Ⓦ www.museicapitolini.org,
Bus Piazza Venezia

Galleria Nazionale d'Arte This museum on the grounds of
the Villa Borghese holds the most important collection of
modern art in Italy, including significant works by Van Gogh,
Degas, Monet, and Cezanne. **Admission:** regular €6; reduced
€3.50. **Hours:** 8:30 A.M. to 7:30 P.M. Tuesday through Sunday;
closed Mondays, January 1 and 2, and December 25 through 27.
Ⓐ Via Barberini 18, Ⓣ 06 32810, Ⓦ www.galleriaborghese.it/
barberini, Ⓜ Spagna

Galleria Nazionale d'Arte Moderna Offering a perfect
follow-up to a visit to the Galleria Nazionale d'Arte, these
exhibits carry the story of modern art through the twentieth
century, with important works by Kandinsky, Miró, Pollack,
Rodin, and Braque. Traveling exhibitions showcase
contemporary Italian painters as well. **Admission:** regular
€9; reduced €7. **Hours:** 8:30 A.M. to 7:30 P.M. Tuesday through
Sunday; closed Mondays. Ⓐ Viale delle Belle Arti 131,
Ⓣ 06 32 2981, Ⓦ www.gnam.arti.beniculturali.it, Ⓜ Spagna

Museo e Galleria Borghese Perhaps the most famous
museum in Rome, the Galleria Borghese houses six
Caravaggio paintings—the most gathered in one place in
all of Italy. Also here are excellent examples of works by
Raphael, Titian, and Bernini. The bookstore and gift shop
have the city's best selection of postcards and art souvenirs.
Admission: regular €8.50; reduced €5.25. **Hours:** 9 A.M. to 7 P.M.
Tuesday through Sunday; closed Mondays, January 1, and
December 25. Ⓐ Piazza Scipione Borghese 5, Ⓣ 06 841 3979,
Ⓦ www.galleriaborghese.it, Ⓜ Spagna

Museo Nazionale Etrusco di Villa Giulia The world's
most comprehensive collection of Etruscan history, art,
and artifacts is housed in this sixteenth-century papal
palace. Included in the exhibits are the tombs of Cerveteri, a
discovery central to the story of the city's pre-Roman culture.
Admission: regular €4; reduced €2. **Hours:** 8:30 A.M. TO 7:30 P.M.
Tuesday through Sunday; closed Mondays. Ⓐ Piazzale di
Villa Giulia 9, Ⓣ 06 320 1951, Tram Viale di Belle Arti

Vatican Museums Scattered across many museums,
the Vatican collections comprise some of the world's
most famous works of art. The most popular destination
in the massive compound is the Sistine Chapel, home to
Michelangelo's brilliant frescoes and stunning ceiling.
Other important sections include a gallery of Rafael's work,
an Etruscan museum, an Egyptian museum, and a gallery

of maps of Italy and the papal territories from 1580. You'll need an entire day—or more—just to scratch the surface. **Admission:** regular €12; reduced €8; free on the last Sunday of each month. **Hours:** 10 A.M. to 3:30 P.M. (summer); 10 A.M. to 12:30 P.M. (off season). Be sure to check the Vatican Museums' website before visiting—galleries are closed several days each month, and hours can change from day to day. Ⓐ Viale Vaticani, Ⓣ 06 6988 3332, Ⓦ www.vatican.va, Ⓜ Ottaviano/San Pietro

GUIDED SIGHTSEEING TOURS

Rome is a city that begs to be wandered—whether you have a purpose or just want to take in the sights—and there's no substitute for exploring the city on your own. A guided tour can, however, provide a quick overview of the highlights, albeit at a fairly high price. Check out these possibilities.

Avventure Bellissime This is a good choice if you're looking for a smaller, more personal experience. Limited to eight people, the three-hour tours are conducted in English and focus on a variety of themes, such as underground Rome or Baroque piazzas and fountains. Prices start at about €60. Ⓦ www.tours-italy.com

Enjoy Rome One of the most popular outfits, Enjoy Rome offers several English-language tours for groups of up to twenty-five. Prices start at €18. Contact the company to arrange specialized tours focused on a particular artist (such as Bernini) or theme (such as fascist architecture). Ⓦ www.enjoyrome.com

Green Line Tours This company offers options such as three-hour tours of Imperial Rome (€32) and Christian Rome (€38), or excursions to Tivoli (€50) and Roman Castles (€38). Ⓦ www.romeguide.it/greenline

Viator Viator runs a three-hour walking tour of ancient Rome (starting at €24) and a full-day tour to Naples and Pompeii (starting at €110). It also operates a fleet of double-decker tour buses (starting at €16). Ⓦ www.viator.com

PERFORMING ARTS

Rome's performing-arts scene is vibrant and varied. Roman opera tends to be traditional and successful, while dance performances tend to be experimental and of more variable quality. Dramatic theater also takes many forms, from classic plays to works by emerging artists. Always ask about student discounts when you buy tickets. For comprehensive listings of performing-arts events in Rome, go to www.charta.it.

OPERA

Teatro dell'Opera di Roma hosts performances by Italy's national opera company as well as by traveling companies from all over the world from November through June. Discounted tickets are available at the box office—just present your student ID. (Cheap tickets can also be had if you're willing to endure hours in the standing-room-only section.) In the summer months, operas are performed in the ruins of Terme di Caracalla, ancient Roman baths that serve as a spectacular setting for outdoor entertainment.

Teatro dell'Opera Ⓐ Piazza Beniamino Gigli 8, Ⓣ 06 48 1601, Ⓦ www.opera.roma.it, Ⓜ Repubblica

Terme di Caracalla Ⓐ Biale delle Terme di Caracalla 52, Ⓣ 06 574 5748, Ⓜ Circo Máximo

BALLET AND DANCE

Rome's foremost ballet venue is the Teatro dell'Opera di Roma (which also doubles as Rome's foremost opera venue). If you're a dance fan, you'll find many places to enjoy world-class performances, including the Teatro Nazionale (Rome's national theater), Giardino do Sisto V (for outdoor performances), Teatro Olimpico (for mainstream and experimental dance), and Spazio Danza (for modern dance). For the most part, the major venues for modern dance are also the major venues for ballet. Here are the most important ones.

Accademia Tedesca a Villa Massimo Ⓐ Largo Villa Massimo 1, Ⓣ 06 442 5931, Ⓦ www.villamassimo.de, Bus Via Tiburtina

Giardino do Sisto V Ⓐ Piazza San Salvatore in Lauro 15, Ⓜ Cipro–Musei Vaticani

Spazio Danza Ⓐ Via Del Monte Della Farina 19, Ⓣ 06 6880 5454, Bus Ponte Garibaldi

Teatro Nazionale Ⓐ Via del Viminale 51, Ⓣ 06 4782 4222, Bus Nazionale

Teatro Olimpico Ⓐ Piazza Gentile di Fabriano 17, Ⓣ 06 323 4936, Ⓦ www.teatroolimpico.it, Bus/Tram Piazza Manzini

Teatro Sistina Ⓐ Via Sistina 129, Ⓣ 06 420 0711, Ⓦ www.ilsistina.com, Ⓜ Barberini

THEATER

You won't find a centralized theater district in Rome. Instead, theaters large and small are scattered throughout the city. If you're hankering for a musical, hit Teatro Sistina, where you'll find big shows—including some you'll recognize, such as *Cabaret*—performed in Italian. If you're seeking smaller-scale classic or contemporary productions, you'll find more options, such as Teatro Belli and Teatro Colosseo, which put on classic plays in Italian, and Teatro Argentina, which offers classic and avant-garde productions. For theater in English, check out the English-language troupes The Emperors of Rome and Shakespeare in the Park.

The Emperors of Rome Ⓐ Via dei Fori Imperiali, near the entrance to the Roman Forum, Ⓦ www.miracleplayers.org, Ⓜ Colosseo

Il Sistina Ⓐ Via Sistina 129, Ⓣ 06 482 6841, Ⓦ www.ilsistina.com, Ⓜ Barberini

Shakespeare in the Park Ⓐ various locations, Ⓦ www.ishakespeare.net

Teatro Argentina Ⓐ Largo di Torre Argentina 52, Ⓣ 06 6880 4061, Bus/Tram Largo di Torre Argentina

Teatro Belli Ⓐ Piazza S. Apollonia 11/A, Ⓣ 06 589 4875, Ⓦ www.teatrobelli.it, Tram Piazzo Sonnino

Teatro Colosseo Ⓐ Via Capo'd'Africa 5/A, Ⓣ 06 700 4932, Ⓦ www.teatrocolosseo.it, Ⓜ Spagna

CLASSICAL MUSIC

Classical music has finally found a respectable Roman home at Renzo Piano's long-awaited Auditorium, a beautiful complex north of the city. Other good places to catch chamber or orchestral music are Teatro Ghione and Aula Magna dell'Universita in Sapienza. The latter two are best for small and local performances, whereas Piano's elaborate spaces draw international musicians.

Auditorium Ⓐ Via P. de Coubertin 15, Ⓣ 06 80242, Ⓦ www.musicaperroma.it, Bus Auditoria

Aula Magna dell'Universita in Sapienza Ⓐ Piazzale Aldo Moro, Ⓣ 06 361 0051, Ⓦ www.concertiiuc.it, Ⓜ Policlinico

Teatro Ghione Ⓐ Via della Fornaci 37, Ⓣ 06 637 2294, Ⓦ www.ghione.it, Ⓜ Cipro–Musei Vaticani

HELLO TICKET

Despite the funny name, the vendor Hello Ticket is your best source for discounted admissions to a variety of Roman venues. Tickets are available for the performing arts as well as for sporting events.

....

Hello Ticket Ⓐ Stazione Termini (near Platform #23), Ⓣ 00 907 080, Ⓜ Termini

FILMS

Italian film is world famous for a reason. In the Fellini era, arguably the heyday of Italian cinema, filmmakers both serious and satirical crafted a paradoxical view of the world. Contemporary Italian cinema is a bit more mainstream, and the most commercially successful films that make money look suspiciously like American blockbusters. Still, a strong contingent of independent filmmakers carry on the Italian tradition. Well-known movies filmed in Rome include *La Dolce Vita* (1960), *Mamma Roma* (1962), *Roma* (1972), and *Caro Diario* (1993). For comprehensive film listings, pick up a copy of *Roma C'è* or visit www.romace.it.

MOVIE THEATERS

Finding English-language films in Rome can be tricky. Plenty of American, British, and Australian films make their way to the city—Romans love American film, in particular—but they're almost always dubbed into Italian. Rome does, however, have four theaters that show films in their original languages, with subtitles. Tickets usually cost €6–€10 (the Pasquino and Quirinetta offer student discounts). All theaters screen afternoon matinees at reduced prices.

Nuovo Sacher Ⓐ Largo Ascianghi 1, Ⓣ 06 581 8116, Bus Via Marmorata

Pasquino Ⓐ Piazza Sant'Edigio, Ⓣ 06 580 3622, Tram Piazza Sonnino

Quirinetta Ⓐ Via M. Minghetti 4, Ⓣ 06 679 0012, Ⓜ Spagna

Warner Village Moderno Ⓐ Piazza della Repubblica 45, Ⓣ 06 4777 9202, Ⓜ Repubblica

FILM FESTIVALS

Summer is the season for film festivals, many of them held outdoors. The classics seem to get equal billing with the indies, so pick according to your pleasure. Although festival types have remained consistent for a number of years, locations and sponsors often change. Be sure to check ahead for details.

Isola del Cinema (July–August) This small festival highlights independent, often local, films. Ⓣ 06 583 3113

Massenzio (July–August) This international (mostly European) festival tends to attract left-wing intellectuals. The focus changes every year—recent themes have included love, war, and history. Ⓣ 06 4281 4962

Notti di Cinema a Piazza di Vittorio (August–September) This festival is a great opportunity to catch first-run Italian films and new European releases. Ⓦ www.agisanec.lazio.it

Sotto le Stelle di San Lorenzo (July–September) This festival is devoted mostly to classic Italian films from the 1950s and 1960s. Ⓣ 06 996 2946

LANGUAGE CLASSES

Improving your Italian or picking up another language can be a great way to spend your free time, gain an invaluable skill, and make new friends. Two-week, forty-hour courses will generally cost up to €400, but prices depend on the frequency of class meetings, the size of the class, and the level of instruction. Here are a few places to consider.

Centro Linguistico Italiano Dante Alighieri Italian Ⓦ www.clidante.it

Centro Mediterraneo French, Italian, Portuguese, Spanish Ⓦ www.mediterraneoschool.com

Istituto Dante Alighieri Italian Ⓦ www.languageinitaly.com

Scuola Leonardo da Vinci Italian Ⓦ www.scuolaleonardo.com

Torre di Babele Italian Ⓦ www.torredibabele.com

FESTIVALS AND HOLIDAYS

Perhaps it only *seems* like Italians celebrate year-round. In Italy, many holidays are centered around the Roman Catholic calendar, but as the major cities become more cosmopolitan and international, festivals are becoming more secular. In addition to Christmas day, New Year's day, and Easter Sunday, Italians enjoy eight major celebrations:

Befana (Epiphany): January 6 For Italian children, the Epiphany is as important as Christmas. Befana is a good witch who bestows gifts—she's the Italian version of Santa Claus.

Venerdì Santo (Good Friday): April The pope presides over this important religious observation, officially blessing the crowd at St Peter's Basilica. The holiday also has a secular version: During the Festa della Primavera, usually landing on or around April 21, the Spanish Steps are adorned with huge pots of azaleas and the surrounding Piazza di Spagna is filled with musicians and performances.

Festa di Noantri (Feast of We Others): July Trastevere's big culinary event gathers foodies and wine lovers to sample recipes from some of the city's best chefs. The main action takes place in Piazza Santa Maria.

Passetto di Borgo: July–August For two weeks every summer, Castel Sant'Angelo, the gargantuan round castle that is one of Rome's most prominent visual landmarks, opens its doors at night—providing visitors with unparalleled views of the cityscape. The celebration is named for the underground passageway that connects Castel Sant'Angelo to the Vatican.
Ⓦ www.castelsantangelo.com

Ferragosto (Assumption): August 15 Officially a celebration of the Assumption of the Virgin Mary, this Catholic holiday launches Rome's summer exodus, as the locals temporarily escape the overheated city and their busy work lives.

Estate Romana: June–September This gigantic music and arts festival has featured headliners such as jazz legend Wynton Marsalis and easy-listening icon Yanni in recent years. Concerts are held in Piazza di Spagna, Piazza Navona, and many other outdoor locations. Ⓦ www.estateromana. comune.roma.it

Castelli Romani Harvest Festival: October Just 20 minutes outside the city walls lies one of the area's prime grape-growing regions, Castelli Romani. Harvest tends to come sometime in October, when wineries open their doors to visitors for tours—and tastes from the previous year's casks. Buses go to the area from the Anangina metro station.

Natale (Christmas): December Christmas is a big deal in this Catholic country. Although commercialism has crept into the monthlong celebration, Natale is still primarily a religious holiday, steeped in cultural tradition. Highlights of the season include *presepi* (exhibits of antique Christmas cribs); the midnight mass on Christmas Eve at Basilica di Santa Maria Maggiore; and the Christmas morning mass at St. Peter's, presided over by the pope and open to all.

5 AFFORDABLE DAY TRIPS

1. **Florence:** Museums and great places to shop abound in this city of Michelangelo and the Medici family. Trains run regularly from Stazione Termini. The fast train usually costs €30, but check Trenitalia's website, www.trenitalia.com, for the occasional Happy Train promotion, which will get you there just as quickly for only €10.

2. **Orvieto:** This central-Italian hill town offers myriad treats: a stunning cathedral (even when you think you've seen enough), a sixteenth-century well with an amazing double-helix under ground stairway, and an impressive Etruscan museum. A €12 train ride (see Trenitalia's website for details) will get you there in an hour.

3. **Ostia Antica:** Spend a day at this nearby port town, a preserved ancient city that's cheaper and closer than the legendary Pompeii. Some of the houses and temples are actually better preserved than those in the more famous city. The train from Stazione Piramide to Ostia Antica takes about 30 minutes and requires only a €1 metro ticket.

4. **Ostia Beach:** Ostia's beach is not only the most stunning in Italy, it's also the most convenient. To get there, follow the directions for Ostia Antica.

5. **Tivoli:** In this Roman suburb, take in the impressive fountains at Villa d'Este and get a sense of Emperor Hadrian's love of grandeur at Villa Adriana. Take the metro to Ponte Mammolo, then the blue COTRAL bus to Tivoli. A local orange bus will take you the extra few minutes to Villa Adriana. The hourlong trip costs about €7.

15. Eating Out

A typical Italian meal in a restaurant, whether you go for dinner or lunch, consists of five courses. The *antipasto* (appetizer) will include a selection of cured meats, pickled vegetables, and olives. The *primo* (first course) is usually pasta or risotto but might also be soup. The *secondo* (main course) might be fish, meat, or poultry and is normally accompanied by a *contorno* (side dish) of vegetables. Save room for *dolci* (dessert). Wine is almost always part of the meal.

No matter what kind of restaurant you're looking for—a casual place to hang out with your friends before heading out to the bars or a nice place to impress visiting family members—keep in mind that Italian meals are meant to be savored and lingered over. Be prepared for meals that go on for hours—and count yourself lucky that you're in a city known the world over for its incredible food.

Throughout this chapter, the symbol ⊘ indicates moderately priced spots where you can expect to spend €10 or less for lunch and about €15 for dinner (a main course plus a drink). Be aware that eating cheaply will be almost impossible if you order multiple courses.

DINNER WITH FRIENDS

Even for cash-strapped students, going out to dinner a couple of times a week is not impossible. Many restaurants cater specifically to the student crowd. The places listed here tend to be less expensive, more casual, and a bit louder than traditional Roman restaurants—they're all good places to catch up with friends or get together before venturing out to the bars.

✓ **Da Baffetto** This is one of Rome's best pizza places, and it caters to a young crowd. Expect to wait in line for a table. Ⓐ Via del Governo Vecchio 114, Ⓣ 06 686 1617, Bus Castel Sant'Angelo

✓ **Dar Poeta** Diners can choose from more than thirty varieties at this pizza parlor, one of the best in the city. Ⓐ Vicolo del Bologna 45, Ⓣ 06 588 0516, Bus Via Garibaldi

Miro The specialty here is fiery cuisine from southern Italy, mostly the region of Calabria. Ⓐ Via dei Banchi Nuovi 8, Ⓣ 06 6880 8527, Bus Piazza Navona

✓ **Ombre Rosse** This super-casual pub next door to the Pasquino Theater offers good, inexpensive food and beer to a movie-going crowd. If it's warm enough, you can sit outside. Ⓐ Piazza Sant'Egidio 12, Ⓣ 06 588 4155, Tram Piazza Sonnino

✓ **Pannattoni** Specializing in old-school pizza and brusque service, this place is worth every inconvenience. Ⓐ Viale Trastevere 53, Ⓣ 06 580 0919, Tram Piazza Sonnino

✓ **Santa Lucia** Here you'll find healthy (and affordable) contemporary Italian food in one of Rome's most beautiful outdoor dining spaces. Ⓐ Largo Febo 12, Ⓣ 06 6880 2427, Bus Piazza Navona

Supperclub This popular nightclub offers great food—some of it Italian, some of it surprising (try the turnip-and-fennel gazpacho). The cocktails are cool, and the atmosphere is trendy and fun. Ⓐ Via de' Nari 14, Ⓣ 06 6880 7207, Bus Via Aurelia

✓ **Tram Tram** This local favorite in student-friendly San Lorenzo offers inventive, moderately priced Italian food. The décor features pieces of old Roman trams, hence the restaurant's name. Ⓐ Via dei Reti 44, Ⓣ 06 49 0416, Ⓜ Piramide

✓ **Trimani Wine Bar** This enormous wine bar features some of the best antipasti in town. Ⓐ Via Cernaia 37B, Ⓣ 06 446 9630, Bus Via Palestro

TIPPING IN RESTAURANTS

Menu prices may already include a service charge, a *pane e coperto* (bread and cover) charge, or both. The practice, however, is slowly waning: If a menu explicitly states "no service charge," you'll be expected to tip 10 to 15 percent. When in doubt, ask your server whether service is included.

DINNER WITH FAMILY

Playing host to out-of-town guests offers a perfect opportunity to show off your restaurant-choosing savvy. Bypass your usual student haunts and head someplace a bit quieter and nicer. Visiting friends and family—even your picky parents—will appreciate any of the restaurants listed below. All ten of them serve up local cuisine at moderate prices.

Checchino dal 1887 Specializing in Roman offal (organ meats such as brains, hearts, and intestines) and a wide-ranging menu of other regional delights, this is the place to go if you have adventurous eaters in your party. Ⓐ Via di Monte Testaccio 30, ⓣ 06 574 6318, Ⓜ Piramide

Ⓥ **Cul de Sac** This crowded, cozy cafe offers a wide selection of international wine and light pastas, sandwiches, and salads. Ⓐ Piazza di Pasquino 73, ⓣ 06 6880 1094, Tram Piazza Sonnino

Da Gigetto Roman-Jewish cooking is the specialty here. Staples include fresh fish, dried cod, fried artichokes, and cheese, all served in a friendly, laid-back setting. Ⓐ Via del Portico d'Ottavia 21A, ⓣ 06 686 1105, Bus Portico d'Ottavia

Da Paris For another taste of Roman-Jewish cuisine—the whole fish is particularly good—try this quiet, romantic space near the Basilica di Santa Maria in Trastevere. Ⓐ Piazza San Callisto 7A, ⓣ 06 581 5378, Tram Piazza Sonnino

Ditirambo As if healthy Italian food made with local—often organic—produce and meats weren't enough, the breads

and desserts here are all homemade. Ⓐ Piazzadella
Cancellaria 74, Ⓣ 06 687 1626, Bus Campo de' Fiori

Ⓥ **'Gusto** This place offers something for everyone,
including, oddly, homemade french fries. Downstairs is part
cafe, part pizzeria; upstairs is a more upscale restaurant.
Ⓐ Piazza Augusto Imperatore 7/9, Ⓣ 06 322 6273, Bus Piazza
Augusto Imperatore

Piperno Specializing in traditional regional cuisines,
Piperno also offers the best Sunday brunch for miles
around. Try the oxtail stew, ricotta fritters, or *pasta alla
amatriciana* (pasta with tomatoes and bacon). Ⓐ Via Monte
dei Cenci 9, Ⓣ 06 6880 6629, Ⓦ www.ristorantepiperno.com,
Bus Campo de' Fiori

Reef This airy, high-ceilinged restaurant features sushi
as well as a variety of fresh seafood dishes. Ⓐ Piazza
Augusto Imperatore 42, Ⓣ 06 6830 1430, Bus Piazza Augusto
Imperatore

Ⓥ **Ristorante La Buca di Ripetta** Serving up traditional
Roman food in a casual atmosphere, this is one of the most
affordable good restaurants in the area surrounding the
Spanish Steps. Ⓐ Via di Ripetta 36, Ⓣ 06 321 9391, Ⓜ Spagna

La Rosetta Some of the best fresh fish in the city is served
here. Ⓐ Via Rosetta 9, Ⓣ 06 686 1002, Bus Via Nazionale

ROMAN CUISINE 101

Gnocchi (pronounced *nee-yo-kee*) are small potato
dumplings served with sauce. *Agnolotti* (stuffed
pastas) are usually filled with finely ground meat
and served in broth. *Spaghetti* is commonly served
with olive oil, garlic, and hot pepper. *Bucatini* is a
thick, hollow spaghetti. *Abbacchio a scottadito* or
grilled bone-in baby lamb chops, is a popular main
course. *Involtini* are rolled strips of meat, usually medium-rare beef, stuffed with spinach and
cheese and served in tomato sauce. *Fritto misto* is
a mixed fry that often contains fish and vegetables
but can also include brains: If you're squeamish
about organ meats, be sure to ask.

DATE SPOTS

The following recommended restaurants are appropriate choices for romantic occasions. Some are moderately priced; others are suitable for a special (read, expensive) night out. They all have in common soft lighting, low-key ambiance, and other ingredients to help you get your romance on.

Antico Arco For contemporary cuisine and excellent service in an elegant space, try this hangout popular with students and academics (the American Academy and the American University of Rome are nearby). Ⓐ Piazzale Aurelio 7, Ⓣ 06 581 5274, Bus Piazzale Aurelio

Asinocotto The only openly gay-owned and -operated restaurant in the city, Asinocotto (literally, *cooked donkey*) was awarded a Michelin star for the excellence of its upscale Italian dishes. Ⓐ Via dei Vascellari 48, Ⓣ 06 589 8985, Bus Ponte Palatino

Ostriche a Colazione Locals come here for updated Italian dishes. The name, literally translated, means *oysters for breakfast.* Ⓐ Via dei Vascellari 21, Ⓣ 06 589 8896, Bus Ponte Palatino

La Pergola The most lauded fine-dining restaurant in Rome is located on the top floor of the Cavalieri Hilton, which crowns Monte Mario. It offers excellent creative Italian cuisine, not to mention the spectacular views. In the summer, there's outside seating for some al fresco romance. Ⓐ Via Cadlolo 101, Ⓣ 06 3509 2211, Ⓦ www.cavalieri-hilton.it, Bus Via Cadlolo

Riparte Café The international cuisine here includes sushi, pasta, and fresh fish. The cafe is inside the hip Ripa Hotel. Ⓐ Via degli Orti di Trastevere 1, Ⓣ 06 58611, Ⓦ www.riparte.com, Bus degli Orti di Trastevere

Sora Lella This unassuming, affordable, candlelit, and multilevel trattoria—on an island in the Tiber, no less—serves traditional Roman food. Ⓐ Via Ponte Quattro Capi 16, Ⓣ 06 686 1601, Tram Piazza Belli

La Terrazza dell'Eden This pricey restaurant in the famous Hotel Eden boasts unbeatable views of Rome along with its menu of spectacular Mediterranean food. Ⓐ Via Ludovisi 49, Ⓣ 06 47 8121, Ⓦ www.hotel-eden.it, Ⓜ Spagna

Testa This wine bar and restaurant is best described as suburban chic: It's out of the city center but filled with hipsters. It features Italian food at moderate prices and is very popular with locals. Ⓐ Via Tirso 30, Ⓣ 06 8530 0692, Bus Villa Borghese

La Veranda del'Hotel Columbus In a gorgeous outdoor space lit up with tiki torches, this restaurant serves up sweeping views of Rome along with upscale Italian and traditional Roman dishes. Ⓐ Borgo Santo Spirito 73, Ⓣ 06 687 2973, Ⓦ www.hotelcolumbus.net, Ⓜ Vaticano

Vineria Reggio This hip wine bar and cafe sits right on the Campo de' Fiori. Drinks are on the cheap side, while food is moderately priced. Ⓐ Campo de' Fiori 15, Ⓣ 06 6880 3268, Bus Campo de' Fiori

> ### *NESSUN FUMARE* (NO SMOKING)
> Eating out in Italy is no longer synonymous with immersing yourself in a smoky fog. As of January 2005, smoking is officially banned in all public places throughout Italy, including bars and restaurants. You can be fined up to €275 if you light up (double that if you're caught smoking near kids or expectant mothers).

VEGETARIAN

You'll find plenty of vegetarian and vegan options in Rome. Order carefully in regular restaurants, though: Much of the regional cuisine is meat-based (we're talking *serious* meat—organs of all kinds are staples of Italian cooking). To locate vegetarian-friendly restaurants and shops throughout Rome and the rest of Europe, visit www.happycow.net. Here are few popular spots.

Arancia Blu This is a trendy, upscale, lacto-ovo joint in San Lorenzo. Ⓐ Via dei Latini 55/65, Ⓣ 06 445 4105, Bus Via Tiburtina

Bio e Te This popular student hangout has a large vegan menu. Ⓐ Via di San Francesco di Sales 1A, Ⓣ 06 6880 9989, Ⓜ Spagna

Il Gelatone For vegans, there's a wide selection of soy gelato at this popular shop. Ⓐ Via dei Serpenti 28, Ⓣ 06 428 0187, Ⓜ Cavour

Il Margutta Vegetariano The menu at this mainstream vegetarian restaurant also caters to omnivores. Ⓐ Via Margutta 118, Ⓣ 06 3265 0577, Ⓜ Flaminio, Spagna

---

PIZZA, ITALIAN-STYLE

In Italy, a pizza is usually about 12 inches in diameter and almost always comes unsliced. The crust is generally of the thin and crispy variety. While it may look like a lot of food, the thin crust keeps the pie from being overly filling, and custom dictates that people don't share pizzas this size.

LATE NIGHT FOOD

The best place for a late-night bite in Rome is a bar that serves food along with the drinks. Most restaurants stop serving by midnight, but some bars are taking up the slack with light menus available until 3:00 A.M. or 4:00 A.M. There aren't very many to choose from, though. If you're hungry late at night, try Da Baffetto (listed in the "Lunch/Food to Go" section) or Supperclub (listed in the "Dinner with Friends" section), or seek out one of the options listed on the next page.

⊘ **Bar del Fico** The snacks are inexpensive and the atmosphere is casual. This place bustles with young people late into the night and features a lively outdoor terrace.
Ⓐ Piazza del Fico 27, Ⓣ 06 686 5205, Bus Piazza Navona

Riparte Café Cap off a night of bar- or club-hopping at this cool space with top-notch food. Ⓐ Via degli Orti di Trastevere 1, Ⓣ 06 58611, Bus Via degli Orti di Trastevere

Cornettificio Sorchetta Doppio Schizzo This all-night pastry shop—a rarity in Rome—serves amazing cornetti. It doesn't have a sign, so look carefully. Ⓐ Via Cernaia 49, Ⓜ Repubblica

LUNCH/FOOD TO GO

Lunch in Rome tends to be a long affair—allow at least two hours if you plan to eat in a restaurant. You can't order takeout from restaurants, so if you're planning a picnic, you'll need to hit up a deli or a market (or the occasional cafe). Popular picnic spots include the banks of the Tiber River, Villa Doria Pamphilj, and Janiculum Hill. Here are some recommended lunch options.

⊘ **Grappolo d'Oro** Inexpensive, traditional Roman food
Ⓐ Piazza della Cancelleria 80, Ⓣ 06 689 7080, Bus Piazza Navona

⊘ **Non Solo Pizza** Serves pizza by the slice (a rarity in Rome) as well as soups, sandwiches, and salads.
Ⓐ Via degli Scipioni 95, Ⓣ 06 372 5820, Ⓜ Spagna

Rosati A good choice for traditional Italian food and excellent people watching, smack in the middle of the action on Piazza del Popolo. Ⓐ Piazza del Popolo 5, Ⓣ 06 322 5859, Ⓜ Piazza del Popolo

Settimio all'Arancio A homey restaurant with excellent Italian comfort food, such as pasta, fried artichokes, fish, and desserts. Ⓐ Via dell'Arancio 50, Ⓣ 06 687 6119, Ⓜ Spagna

Shaki A contemporary cafe near the Spanish Steps that specializes in healthy updates of traditional Italian pastas. Ⓐ Via Mario dei Fiori 29A, Ⓣ 06 678 9244, Ⓜ Spagna

Ⓥ **Tazza d'Oro** Serves some of the best espresso in all of Italy, panini to go, and coffee or tea to send to friends back home. Ⓐ Via d'Orfani 84, 29A, Ⓣ 06 678 9792, Ⓦ www.tazzadorocoffeeshop.com, Bus Piazza Navona

Ⓥ **Trattoria Ugo e Maria** A small, family-owned restaurant that offers large portions of traditional Roman fare at low prices (rumor has it that Mussolini was a patron). Ⓐ Via dei Prefetti 19, Ⓣ 06 687 3752, Ⓜ Spagna

Ⓥ **Volpetti** The most famous deli in Rome, with all the ingredients for an Italian picnic, including excellent cheese and bread. Ⓐ Via Marmorata 47, Ⓣ 06 5730 1439, Ⓦ www.volpetti.com, Ⓜ Piramide

Ⓥ **Zi' Fenizia** The only restaurant in Rome that serves kosher pizza. Ⓐ Via Mario dei Fiori 29A, Ⓣ 06 678 9244, Tram Via Arenula

5 *ALMOST* FREE WAYS TO SPEND AN EVENING WITH FRIENDS

1. **The Spanish Steps:** Join the hoards of tourists and enjoy some of Rome's choicest people-watching. Just be careful: The steps get hot enough in the summer to burn bare legs. Ⓜ Spagna

2. **Janiculum Hill:** Trek up the hill's staircases and hunker down in the Piazzale Garibaldi. Gossip while the sun sets, and see if you can spot the Pantheon's dome from the overlook. Bus Via Garibaldi

3. **Castel Sant-Angelo:** Take in the view from the famous castle's roof bar. On some evenings, you can enter the bar without paying admission to the castle (€5). Bus Piazza Pia

4. **Play cards:** Scrounge up some spare change for bets, then grab some Italian friends and have them teach you how to play cards with an Italian deck. Italian decks usually have forty cards, with four suits that vary by region: coins or suns, swords, cups, and clubs or batons.

5. **Free concerts:** Scour *Roma C'è* (an entertainment guide you can buy at any newsstand) for free concert listings.

16. Night Life

I n Rome, the night scene heats up at 9:00 P.M. or 10:00 P.M., the magic hour when the dinner bills are requested and the barhopping begins. Most older Romans go about this ritual in their own neighborhoods, but young people often head out to a few destination bars. Bars and clubs typically stay open until 12:00 A.M. on weeknights and 2:00 A.M. on weekends— in some neighborhoods, the party goes on till dawn.

Many Roman bars are actually cafes. By day, they serve coffee and lunch; at night, they transform into people-watching and partying spots, especially in the night life hubs where they're most concentrated (Campo de' Fiori, San Lorenzo, and Piazza Navona). In keeping with Rome's general lack of pretension, there isn't a particular look needed to get into a happening bar or club. While there are plenty of fashionistas of both sexes around, you'll be welcome if you pay the cover charge.

> In this chapter, ✅ indicates clubs and live-music venues that don't (or sometimes don't) charge a cover. In these places, how much you spend depends on how much you drink.

BARS

In most Roman bars, you'll find yourself drinking alongside local residents and savvy visitors. The best places to find a young, lively crowd are in Campo de' Fiori, Trastevere, and Via di Monte Testaccio. Campo de' Fiori always offers a surprising mix of both tourists and the hip locals hoping to meet them, Trastevere tends to be populated by Brits and Americans, and Via di Monte Testaccio has the most local vibe. Here are a few reliable bets for a fun night out.

Anima Welcomes beautiful people from all over the world, with a lively DJ, comfortable seating (think beds and couches), and killer cocktails. Ⓐ Via di Santa Maria dell'Anima 8, Ⓣ 06 86 4661, Ⓜ Cipro–Musei Vaticani

Bar del Fico Features a good wine list and inexpensive snacks in a casual atmosphere that attracts young people hoping for prime space on the terrace. Ⓐ Piazza del Fico 27, Ⓣ 06 686 5205, Bus Piazza Navona

The Drunken Ship American-owned, with a downscale, casual environment and cool cocktails for young people on a budget. Ⓐ Campo de' Fiori 20, Ⓣ 06 6830 0535, Ⓦ www.drunkenship.com, Bus Campo de' Fiori

Fiddler's Elbow The oldest traditional Irish pub in the city (it opened in 1976), serving a variety of beers on tap. Ⓐ Via dell'Olmata 43, Ⓣ 06 487 2110, Ⓦ www.thefiddlerselbow.com, Bus Via Giovanni Lanza

Riparte Café Offers a contemporary, neon red–lit atmosphere in the hip Ripa Hotel. Ⓐ Via degli Orti di Trastevere 1, Ⓣ 06 58611, Ⓦ www.riparte.com, Bus Via degli Orti di Trastevere

Stravinskij Bar (in the Hotel de Russie) A celebrity magnet that serves up sightings of stars such as Julianne Moore and Heidi Klum along with swank cocktails. Ⓐ Via del Babuino 9, Ⓣ 06 21 8881, Ⓦ www.russiehotel.com, Ⓜ Flaminio

Swing A piano bar, inside the club Gilda, that draws international musicians as well as a quiet, multinational crowd. Ⓐ Via Mario dei Fiori 97, Ⓣ 06 678 4838, Ⓜ Spagna

La Terrazza dell'Eden bar (in the Hotel Eden) A chic, expensive bar with pricey cocktails to match the glamorous atmosphere—lush upholstered chairs in front of gigantic picture windows that provide amazing panoramic views of the city. Ⓐ Via Ludovisi 49, Ⓣ 06 47 8121, Ⓦ www.hotel-eden.it, Ⓜ Spagna

Vineria Reggio A trendy wine bar and cafe right on the Campo de' Fiori, an ideal spot for people watching, day and night. Ⓐ Piazza Campo de' Fiori 15, Ⓣ 06 6880 3268, Bus Campo de' Fiori

> ## TIPPING IN BARS
>
> In bars—unlike restaurants—tipping follows strict guidelines. In most bars, you should tip 10 percent for good service. Regulars tend simply to round up the bill to the nearest €1 or €5 if it's a nice place. In dives or student bars, however, tipping isn't expected.

CLUBS

One of the beauties of clubbing in Rome is that no matter what your scene is, you'll be welcome—you won't find any velvet ropes here. Venues host a variety of crowds and types of music, and cover charges vary, depending on the night, the DJ, and other factors. In general, expect to pay a cover ranging from €15 to €20 (the charge usually includes a drink). Here are some perennially popular places to check out.

Akab Cave One of the brightest lights on Monte Testaccio Row (Rome's largest concentration of clubs), but designed like a cave inside, with dark lighting and stone walls; features DJs who spin mostly alternative and world music. Ⓐ Via di Monte Testaccio 69, Ⓣ 06 575 7494, Ⓦ www.akabcave.com, Ⓜ Piramide

Alien Features mainly American bands and welcomes a young crowd that is predominantly heterosexual during the week and more overtly gay on the weekends. Ⓐ Via Velletri 13, Ⓣ 06 841 2212, Bus Nomentana

Bush Offers some of Rome's best techno—and the most likely place for spotting someone with blue or orange hair alongside a middle-aged guy in a suit and tie. Ⓐ Via Galvani 46, Ⓣ 06 5728 8691, Ⓜ Piramide

Caruso Café de Oriente Draws a big crowd with Latin American bands and dancing; often expensive to get in, but offers free salsa lessons on Monday nights. Ⓐ Via di Monte Testaccio 36, Ⓣ 06 574 5019, Ⓦ www.carusocafedeoriente.com, Ⓜ Piramide

Supperclub A super-trendy club known for serving drinks—and dinner—in bed. Ⓐ Via de'Nari 14, Ⓣ 06 6880 7207, Ⓦ www.supperclub.com, Bus Pantheon

LIVE MUSIC

Rome has only a handful of established live-music venues, but they've stood the test of time and represent all imaginable tastes. Many international bands come through the city on their way to Paris or from London, so the headliners often show up in Roman clubs on weeknights. Ticket prices vary and often are very affordable; contact individual venues for details.

Alexanderplatz This jazz club is regarded as the city's best. The music begins every night at 10:00 P.M. Membership is required for admission, but costs only €10 per month or €30 per year. Ⓐ Via Ostia 9, Ⓣ 06 3974 2171, Ⓦ www.alexanderplatz.it, Ⓜ Cipro–Musei Vaticani

✅ **Alpheus** This affordable club features live music on four stages every weekend and DJs throughout the week. Students are admitted free on Wednesdays; cover charges vary other nights of the week. Friday nights draw a largely gay crowd. Ⓐ Via del Commercio 36, Ⓣ 06 574 7826, Bus Via Ostiense

Big Mama This small, always crowded club stages live jazz and blues acts, singer-songwriters, and much more. A membership card (€13 per year) is required for admission; additional ticket charges sometimes apply. Visit the website for details. Ⓐ Vicolo di San Francesco A. Ripa 18, Ⓣ 06 581 2551, Ⓦ www.bigmama.it, Tram Piazza Sonnino

Bluecheese Factory Mostly British and American bands are hosted in this former bocce arena turned concert hall. Tickets are cheap, usually less than €5. (Ⓐ) Via Caio Cestio 513, (Ⓣ) 06 5725 0032, (Ⓜ) Piramide

Caffé Latino This is Rome's best spot for live music from Central and South America (when there are no live acts scheduled, there's a DJ and dancing). It draws a crowd of mostly thirty-somethings, and the cover is usually less than €10. (Ⓐ) Via di Monte Testaccio 96, (Ⓣ) 06 5728 8586, (Ⓜ) Piramide

Dome Rock Café The crowd is mostly British, and the selection of beers on tap is extensive. Alternative London bands are the focus. (Ⓐ) Via Domenico Fontana 18, (Ⓣ) 06 7045 2436, Bus Viale Manzoni

Jazz Café Live jazz every night (except Mondays) draws a subdued, intellectual crowd. (Ⓐ) Via Zanardelli 12, (Ⓣ) 06 686 1990, Bus Piazza Navona

Il Locale Some of the best local Italian bands get their big breaks here. (Ⓐ) Vicolo del Fico 3, (Ⓣ) 06 687 9075, Bus Piazza Navona

Micca Club This multifunctional club is part lounge, part concert venue, and part dance club. (Ⓐ) Via Pietra Micca 7/A, (Ⓣ) 06 8744 0079, (Ⓦ) www.miccaclub.com, (Ⓜ) Termini

I Vitelloni This no-frills dive offers cheap drinks and loud bands, most of whom hail from other E.U. countries. (Ⓐ) Via di San Giovanni in Laterano 142, (Ⓣ) 06 7447 8167, Bus Via Merulana

DRINKING LEGALLY

The legal drinking age in Italy is sixteen. Whether you're buying alcohol in a bar, a liquor store, or a supermarket, you'll rarely be asked for ID.

GAY/LESBIAN BARS AND CLUBS

Gay and lesbian culture isn't exactly front and center in Rome, but plenty of venues welcome a gay clientele. Most commonly, nightclubs that draw a primarily heterosexual crowd will devote a night or two specifically to gay patrons. Of the bars and clubs listed earlier in this chapter, Anima, Alien, Akab, and Alpheus are particularly open to partiers of all orientations. Other bars and clubs worth checking out are listed here. For comprehensive gay listings—including night life, entertainment, and more—check out www.gayrome.com, www.gaytour.it, www.clubclassic.net, or www.gaymap.info/rome.

La Buca di Bacco A lounge/bar that welcomes gays and lesbians with an open attitude, great cocktails, and light food. Ⓐ Via di San Francesco a Ripa 165, Ⓣ 348 764 7388, Bus Via Portuense

Coming Out A laid-back gay pub that is an excellent place to start an evening out. Ⓐ Via San Giovanni in Laterano 8, Ⓣ 06 700 9871, Ⓜ Colosseo

Ⓥ **L'Hangar** An American-owned gay club with a focus on fetish and leather and a cover charge of one drink; always crowded with young people. Ⓐ Via In Selci 69, Ⓣ 06 4881 3971, Ⓜ Cavour

OTHER ACTIVITIES

Even die-hard partiers need a break from clubbing and barhopping. The following activities aren't necessarily popular among Romans, but you might find them to be a good way to make new American or international friends.

Bowling There's only one bowling alley, Playland, within the city center. Ⓐ Via Cavour 333, Ⓣ 06 679 0309, Bus Via Nazionale

Comedy Aficionados won't want to miss the comedy nights at the Teatro dell'Opera di Roma, where, once a month, the famous opera house gives its stage to comedy troupes from all over Europe. Ⓐ Via Firenze 72, Ⓣ 06 481 9249, Ⓦ www. operaroma.it, Bus Via Nazionale. Teatro Flaino also features comedy every summer weekend, although some of the acts are geared toward children. Ⓐ Via Santo Stefano del Cacco 15, Ⓣ 06 678 1544, Bus Piazza Venezia

Karaoke Although its crowd is strictly international and non-Roman, Il Trillo Parlante hosts the best karaoke in the city. Ⓐ Via Ostia 29, Ⓣ 06 3974 2156, Ⓜ Cipro–Musei Vaticani

5 COOL DRINKS YOU WON'T FIND AT YOUR COLLEGE BAR BACK HOME

1. **Frangelico, Amaro, and Sambuca:** These after-dinner drinks are all local favorites. Hazelnut-flavored Frangelico and bitter Amaro are often mixed with coffee, while anise-flavored Sambuca is sometime served *con la mosca* (with the fly), with three coffee beans floating in the glass.

2. **Limoncello:** Strong and sweet, this powerful lemon liqueur is a popular after-dinner drink served on its own, rather than with a mixer.

3. **Grappa:** Steel yourself and try some grappa, which looks like vodka but is made from the distilled skins, stems, and seeds of grapes. It's usually 80 or 100 proof—drink slowly! Grappa is typically served straight (in a small glass) as an after-dinner drink, but some Italians like to mix it with their espresso.

4. **Coffee-flavored liqueur:** Italy is a coffee capital: As you might expect, coffee-flavored liqueur is ubiquitous. Try it at Sant'Eustachio, one of Rome's best espresso shops. Ⓐ San' Eustachio 82, ☎ 06 6880 2048, Bus Largo Torre Argentino

5. **Nonalcoholic drinks:** Try a red orange juice or an almond milk—both are nonalcoholic Italian specialties.

VITAVECC.
8:27 9
LBANO LAZ.
8:30 2
APOLI C.LE
REG
8:32
ILANO C.LE
REG
8:35 18
8:47
APOLI C.LE
REG
8:35 27
IUMICINO A.
8:40 15
VENEZIA S. L
8:45
VELLETRI
DIR
8:47
CIVITAVECC.
DIR
8:49
8:52
8:55
REG
9:00
REG
9:05
informazioni supplementari
VIETATO OLTREPASSARE LA LINEA
PRIMA DEL COMPLETO

17. Going Away

One of the best things about Rome is its proximity to the rest of Europe. Although Italy is set apart from the rest of the continent, jutting out as it does into various seas, the country's network of roads and trains easily connect it to France, Switzerland, Austria, and other not-too-far-away destinations. Just a few hours of travel could bring you through several countries.

Given Italy's excellent and affordable train system, not to mention a proliferation of low-cost airlines, there's no reason not to take advantage of a long weekend here or a week or two there to discover a new city, region, or country. Reserve your tickets far in advance for trips during popular traveling periods (summer, especially August, is high season) to guarantee getting a seat and avoid paying a fortune.

EURAIL

A Eurail pass may be the best option if you want to see many towns, cities, and countries. These popular passes cover trains and ferries and allow deeply discounted travel. Eurail passes are intended for visitors and are not generally sold in Europe, so order your pass before you leave the United States or have one sent to you from home. You can place orders directly from the Eurail website (www.eurail.com) or through an online travel service, such as STA Travel (www.statravel.com).

EURAIL OPTIONS

A basic Eurail pass allows for unlimited travel during a specified period (ranging from fifteen days to three months) and starts at about €400 for travelers aged twenty-five and under. With this pass, you can travel within eighteen European countries, excluding Great Britain and many countries in Eastern Europe and the Balkans. You have several additional options if you can be flexible about your travel dates and destinations. Be aware that the following prices do not include additional costs for high-speed trains, certain ferry lines, and (if you choose comfort over budget) sleeping accommodations on overnight trains. Reservations are mandatory for some high-speed and overnight trains; be sure to book your travel ahead of time during busy vacation periods.

Eurailpass Global Pass Flexi A good choice if you intend to take sporadic trips, the Eurailpass Global Pass Flexi allows pass holders to travel for either ten or fifteen days (consecutive or spread apart) within a two-month period. The cost is between about €600 and €800 for youth and €700 and €940 for adults over twenty-five.

Eurail National Pass A Eurail National Pass allows unlimited travel within Italy's borders for three to ten days (consecutive or spread apart) within a two-month period.

Eurail Select Pass and Eurail Regional Pass A Eurail Select Pass allows travel in three, four, or five bordering countries (selected from a list of twenty-two countries) for a specified number of days within a two-month period. A Eurail Regional Pass allows travel in two neighboring countries for four to ten days within a two-month period. These options can put you out anywhere from €250 to €700 or so, depending on your age and on the number of travel days and countries you choose.

TRENITALIA

Trenitalia, the Italian train system, travels both within and beyond Italy and is a remarkably efficient and economical way to get around. You can purchase tickets at any train station; Stazione Termini has easy-to-use machines with instructions in English. For schedules, fares, and tickets, visit www.trenitalia.com. (See "Trains" in Chapter 3 for additional information on traveling by train in Italy.) Here are some of your options.

Biglietto Flexi This pass allows unlimited, unreserved travel on the Trenitalia system for specified periods of time. Prices are comparable to what you'd pay for a Eurail National pass.

InterCity (IC) and Eurostar (ES) Trains Your best bet for longer trips, these offer the fewest stops but are more expensive than local trains. IC trains serve only Italy, whereas the ES trains serve all of Western Europe's major cities. Be advised that it's always cheaper to buy round-trip tickets than one-way segments—if you don't use a return portion, you can always get a full refund. There are no student discounts.

TRAVELING BY BUS

If you're considering traveling by bus, think carefully about what your comfort and time are worth to you—and remember that Rome is in the middle of Italy, a long bus ride to even the nearest neighboring country. Taking a train or a discount flight is usually affordable, even on a student budget. That said, Eurolines offers bus service to widespread destinations across the European continent for very competitive prices; check the website for more details.

Eurolines ⓣ 05 535 7110, ⓦ www.eurolines.com

AIR TRAVEL

The discount airline industry is flourishing, and new companies connecting Rome to any number of European cities pop up all the time. Keep in mind that these airlines sell tickets for each leg of a trip separately, so you won't save money by purchasing a round-trip ticket. But this may work to your advantage, as it offers more flexibility in building itineraries. You can easily fly into one city, do some traveling by land, then fly back from another city without having to backtrack.

To find out which economy airlines fly from Rome to your destination, check www.flylc.com, a handy site that lets you see every city serviced from your chosen departure airport and which discount airline will get you there. Even Alitalia (www.alitalia.com), Italy's major airline, often has good fares, as it's forced to compete in the discount marketplace. Here are some of the most popular discount airlines that serve Rome.

- Air Berlin Ⓦ www.airberlin.de
- Air Europa Ⓦ www.aireuropa.com
- Air One Ⓦ www.air-one.it
- Bmibaby Ⓦ www.bmibaby.com
- Condor Ⓦ www10.condor.com
- EasyJet Ⓦ www.easyjet.com
- Germanwings Ⓦ www.germanwings.com
- Hapag Lloyd Express Ⓦ www.hlf.de
- Myair Ⓦ www.myair.com
- Norwegian Ⓦ www.norwegian.no
- Ryanair Ⓦ www.ryanair.com
- Sky Europe Ⓦ www.skyeurope.com
- Transavia Ⓦ www.transavia.com
- Vueling Ⓦ www.vueling.com

UNDERSTANDING DISCOUNT FARES

Before you get too excited about great deals—like that one-way flight from Rome to Amsterdam you just found online for less than €1—be aware of these catches:

- **Surcharges:** Taxes and fees can tack an extra €20 or more to an advertised fare. Some outfits will even charge you extra for booking by phone. And take note: Baggage restrictions are harsh, so check the limits before you pack, or you may face steep fees at the airport.

- **Restrictions:** Most sale fares apply exclusively to mid-week travel (Tuesday through Thursday) and may require flying at awkward times. And remember that the number of tickets available at discounted prices is usually limited. Signing up to receive airlines' emailed sale bulletins can give you an edge in the race for cheap seats.

- **Secondary airports:** Discount carriers often cut costs by using smaller, secondary airports, which are often less accessible than the major airports. In Rome, you'll have to fly out of (and into) Ciampino Airport.

PACKAGE TRIPS AND TOURS

All around Rome, you'll see advertisements for all-inclusive package trips to sunny vacation spots like Turkey, Tunisia, or Thailand. You'll also come across ads for package tours that send a group of travelers off with a guide; many of these specialize in outdoor adventures like hiking or rafting.

Package trips and tours generally offer genuine deals: The advertised prices typically include airfare, hotel, and all meals and drinks (they don't include tax, travel insurance, or extra activities). Of course, the destination countries tend to be inexpensive in the first place. Planning a trip yourself should be equally affordable—and you'll enjoy the freedom of choosing your own day-to-day activities.

That said, here are some popular companies that arrange trips and tours.

Bella Vita Italia Popular with students and budget travelers for all kinds of customized tours throughout Italy.
Ⓦ www.bellavitaitalia.com

Buongusto Tours Affordable culinary tours with an emphasis on the Piedmont region in the Northwest of Italy.
Ⓦ www.buongustotours.com

Context Travel Very popular with graduate students for ground itineraries in Italy as well as Paris (airfare not included). Ⓦ www.contexttravel.com

La Dolce Vita Tours Seaside excursions and packages with a focus on outdoor adventures and culinary interests.
Ⓣ 06 52 04 665, Ⓦ www.ladolcevitatours.com

PerilloTours Adventure-travel specialists offering affordable, customized tours of all Italian regions.
Ⓣ (800) 431 1515, Ⓦ www.perillotours.com

A FEW MONEY-SAVING OPTIONS

Here are some discount programs that can help you keep down expenses on an out-of-Rome adventure.

AAA Active members of the American Automobile Association can get discounts on European hotels, restaurants, rental cars, and attractions. Ⓦ www.arceurope.com

Nomads Available through STA Travel and online, a Nomads Adventure Card entitles the holder to discounts at hundreds of hostels throughout Europe, as well as reduced rates for Internet access and phone cards. Ⓦ www.nomadsworld.com

VIP Backpackers A VIP Card will bring you discounts on bus trips, flights, activities, restaurants, and hostels around the globe. It also doubles as a rechargeable phone card. Ⓦ www.vipbackpackers.com

YHA (Youth Hostel Association) You'll need a YHA membership card if you want to stay at one of thousands of youth hostels around Europe and the world operated by Hostelling International. The card can also get you reduced rates at participating hostels in England and Wales. Ⓦ www.yha.org.uk

RENTING A CAR

If you can bear the idea of sharing the road with Italian drivers (see the box on page 188)—renting a car can be a good way to go. In Italy, you must be at least twenty-one years old to rent a car (some companies will add a surcharge if you're between twenty-one and twenty-four; some require a minimum age of twenty-five). A standard-transmission rental should run you about €200 a week, not including tax, gas, and insurance. Note that gasoline is way more expensive in Europe than it is in the United States, and that some major credit cards offer free insurance as a perk (contact your card issuer for details). In Europe, rental cars are almost always stick shifts. If you need an automatic, be sure to request it specifically.

The big names in car rentals—Hertz, Budget, Avis, and Europcar—all have branches at the Rome airports, at Stazione Termini, and at other locations around Rome. EasyCar, the most popular online rental service, generally offers more favorable rates; the catch is that you must pay up front (no refunds) and return the car to the same place where you picked it up. Here are the main car-rental agencies serving Rome and Italy.

- **Auto Europe** Ⓦ www.autoeurope.com
- **Avis** Ⓣ 06 6501 1531, Ⓦ www.avis.com
- **EasyCar** Ⓦ www.easycar.com
- **Europcar** Ⓣ 06 541 0252, Ⓦ www.europcar.com
- **Hertz** Ⓣ 06 650 1553, Ⓦ www.hertz.com
- **Holiday Autos** Ⓣ 199 470 480, Ⓦ www.holidayautos.com
- **Maggiore** Ⓣ 06 6501 0678, Ⓦ www.maggiore.it
- **Tiger Car Rental** Ⓦ www.tigercarrental.com

You can also book a car rental through these general travel websites, which may offer more flexibility in pickup/drop-off locations (and if you use a U.S.-based site, it'll let you pay in dollars).

- Expedia Ⓦ www.expedia.com
- Opodo Ⓦ www.opodo.com
- Orbitz Ⓦ www.orbitz.com
- Travelocity Ⓦ www.travelocity.com

THOSE CRAZY ITALIAN DRIVERS!

Roman drivers are known for being aggressive. Lanes are routinely ignored, and some areas don't have marked lanes at all. If you do rent a car, pack your patience and prepare yourself for some defensive driving. See "Cars and Scooters" in Chapter 3 for more information on driving in Italy, including some general rules of the road.

5 AFFORDABLE WAYS TO SPEND YOUR SPRING OR MIDTERM BREAK

1. **Cheap flights:** Hop on a cheap flight with a discount airline and visit Madrid, Berlin, or another major city. If you're lucky, you can find tickets for as little as €10—sometimes even less.

2. **Rome's free attractions:** Go ahead, be a tourist. The Capitoline and Vatican Museums both waive admission fees on Sundays. Other good, inexpensive sites include the Mausoleo di Augusto in Piazza Augusto Imperatore (Bus Piazza San Silvestro) or the Aula Ottagona, which now houses Roman sculpture but was once part of the ancient baths of Diocletian (Ⓜ Termini).

3. **Art, art, and more art:** Dedicate a day to your favorite artist. Find out where all of Rome's Caravaggio paintings are located (an online search will help) and church- and museum-hop the days away.

4. **Sperlonga:** Head to this beach town halfway between Rome and Naples. You'll have to pony up for a hotel room (about €100 a night for a double), but the €12 round-trip train ticket makes up the difference.

5. **Small towns:** Visit some of the little-known Italian towns that you can reach by train for less than €50. Bergamo, a town near Milan, has a beautiful cathedral and excellent pastry shops. Ravenna, in the Northeast, is famous for its mosaics—and Dante's tomb. Assisi, the beautiful medieval town made famous by St. Francis, has two medieval castles and the St. Francis cathedral.

18. Emergencies

I t's possible that your time in Rome will be the first time you're on your own, not to mention the first time you'll be living in a big city. Although most students can count on their study-abroad programs to assist in times of need, true emergencies require immediate action.

You should know what number to dial for help during a medical or legal emergency. You should also note the hospital and police department closest to where you live. When all is said and done, the type of emergency you're most likely to face is more along the lines of a stolen MP3 player or wallet. Nevertheless, thinking through potential "what if" scenarios in advance can prevent frustration and confusion when you are least prepared to handle them.

IMPORTANT PHONE NUMBERS

If you find yourself in an emergency during your time in Rome, remember one number: 112. This is your all-purpose emergency number, whether you're in need of an ambulance, the police, or firefighters. 112 can be accessed from anywhere in Europe—you'll be connected to local emergency service, just like 911 does in the United States. With its English-speaking operators, this is the best choice for students and other travelers abroad. In this section, we'll provide Rome's local emergency numbers. Just remember that if you call a local number, you many not reach an English-speaking operator.

112 (Europe-wide emergency services number) Call this number from any cell phone or landline to reach medical, police, or fire services; English-speaking operators are available. Be prepared with the address of where you are,

your telephone number, and, if you're calling for someone else, the victim's name and age. For more information, go to www.sos112.info.

MEDICAL EMERGENCIES

Rest assured that in the event of an emergency Italian hospitals will receive you and provide you with excellent care, regardless of the type of insurance you have. But do be sure to check with your insurance provider to find out what emergency care and services it covers—before you're faced with an actual emergency. Ambulance service is free in Italy, even if you don't have insurance. See the "Useful Phrases" section in the Appendix for Italian phrases you can use in the event of an emergency.

113 This is the general emergency number in Italy. Call it from any cell phone or landline when a life-threatening medical condition requires immediate attention. Be prepared with the address of where you are, your telephone number, and, if you're calling for someone else, the victim's name and age.

CALLING THE EMBASSY

A consular officer at the U.S. Embassy can assist you in the event of a medical or other emergency. Services include helping you locate appropriate medical services, contacting family or friends, and arranging a money transfer from a U.S. bank account, if necessary.

06 46741 Call this number, available twenty-four hours a day, to reach the U.S. Embassy in Rome. Listen for the emergency number, which is always on the recorded greeting.

FIRE

Many apartment buildings in Rome are old, which means that escaping during a fire can be a little complicated. Many apartments are without smoke detectors or fire escapes and may be located on the interior of a wide block of apartment buildings. Further, many neighborhoods have narrow streets on which double-parked cars can completely impede all traffic. Don't hesitate to call the fire department immediately in any emergency.

> **115** Call this number from any cell phone or landline to reach the fire department. Be prepared to provide a precise address or location, a telephone number, and the number and condition of any victims.

GAS LEAKS

If you suspect a gas leak, immediately shut off all electrical appliances (including lights, cell phones, and landlines), close the gas valve, and open as many windows as possible before calling (*from outside*) the gas service's emergency number or the fire department. Follow all instructions given to you and don't hang up until you are told to do so.

> **800 803 020** Call this number to reach the gas service's emergency line. (The fire department will also respond to gas leaks).

POLICE

There are two main police branches in Italy: the *polizia* and the *carabinieri*. The *polizia* are governed by the Ministry of the Interior and housed at the local *questura* (state police office) in every Italian city. The *carabinieri,* or neighborhood force, perform both military and civilian duties. Either branch can help you in an emergency, but the *polizia* are the first responders.

---

113 Call this number to report an emergency involving crime or violence. This is Italy's general emergency number; you'll be transferred to a local department if necessary.

ROME SAFETY 101

Here are some tips to help keep you safe during your time in Rome:

- **Blending in:** Thieves target tourists and foreigners, so make sure you're not an easy mark. Examining the metro map in public, shouting in English, and wearing flip-flops and shorts will make you stand out.

- **Pickpockets:** Watch out for pickpockets on the metro, on crowded buses, or in touristy areas such as the Colosseum and the Spanish Steps. If you're in a cafe or restaurant, be sure to keep your cell phone, camera, bag, and other belongings close to you—especially if you're sitting outdoors.

- **Team thieves:** Be wary if children approach you begging for money or offering to play accordion music for you. These kids are there to distract you while another person runs off with your wallet, camera, or bag.

GETTING CITED OR ARRESTED

Chances are good that you'll never have a single interaction with a police officer in Rome. If you do, however, find yourself in trouble with the law, here are some of the rights you're entitled to during custody:

- To know, within twenty-four hours after an arrest, why you're being held

- To consult a lawyer—and to not respond to questioning without an attorney present

- To make a phone call, but only after receiving permission from a presiding judge

If you're arrested, the Italian authorities will contact the U.S. Embassy. The consulate will apply for a visiting permit and send a representative to meet with you within two working days. Representatives can provide a list of local lawyers if needed, help with financial matters, contact family and friends, and answer questions. Their job is to make sure that you are treated fairly under Italian law, in accordance with Italian regulations.

CALLING A LAWYER

Law firms in Italy are highly specialized, and fees vary, so call around. If you don't hear of a good lawyer by word of mouth, search the list of English-speaking lawyers on the U.S. Embassy's website, italy.usembassy.gov.

LOST OR STOLEN PROPERTY

Lost-and-found offices are located in airports and train stations all over Rome. If you're the victim of a theft, immediately report the loss to the police by calling 113. If your wallet is lost or stolen, cancel all of your credit and bank cards as soon as possible. If your cell phone is lost or stolen, call your provider to have your number blocked. If you lose an item on public transportation, call one of the following numbers for help locating it.

ATAC (buses) Ⓐ Via Nicola Bettoni 1, ⓣ 06 581 6040,
Bus **Via Portuense**

COTRAL (metro) Ⓐ Metro Furio Camillo, ⓣ 06 5753 3620,
Ⓜ Furio Camillo

FS (trains) Ⓐ Via Giovanni Giolitti 24, ⓣ 06 4730 6682,
Ⓜ Termini

CANCELING LOST OR STOLEN CREDIT CARDS

Keep a record of your credit card details—issuers, account numbers, and customer service phone numbers—in a safe place. You can also try one of these numbers in the event that your credit card is lost or stolen.

- **American Express (a U.S. number; call collect)** ⓣ 905 474 870
- **MasterCard (Global Service)** ⓣ 800 964 767
- **Visa (International Assistance Center)** ⓣ 800 895 082

REPLACING A PASSPORT

If your passport is stolen, report the theft first to the police and then to the U.S. Embassy. To replace your passport, go in person to the passport office in the embassy's consular section (no appointment is necessary) and bring the items listed below. If you have immediate travel plans, you can get an emergency passport, which can often be issued on the same day you apply. It will be valid for a limited time, cannot be extended, and must be exchanged for a regular passport as soon as you return from your trip. If you don't expect to travel for some time, you can apply for a regular replacement passport, which you will receive in approximately two weeks. You can exchange your emergency passport for a regular passport either in Italy or in the United States.

REPLACEMENT PASSPORT CHECKLIST

Here's what you'll need to bring with you when you apply for a replacement passport:

- ✓ Completed forms DS-11 (Passport Application) and DS-64 (Statement Regarding Lost or Stolen Passport), which you can download at www.travel.state.gov)

- ✓ Two identical passport-size photos (photo machines are available at the consulate for a small fee)

- ✓ Proof of U.S. citizenship, if possible

- ✓ Any form of identification you have, preferably with a photograph

- ✓ Fee payment (currently $97) in cash, money order, or credit card (no checks)

UNEXPECTED TRIPS HOME

Should there be a death in your family or another crisis at home while you're living abroad, airlines can sometimes assist you with securing a last-minute flight to the United States. Each airline has its own policy on how to deal with such situations. Some may offer you a bereavement ticket with a flexible return date—this type of ticket, however, is usually very expensive and often requires proof that an immediate family member has died. You can almost always find cheaper last-minute fares yourself simply by searching general travel websites such as www.orbitz.com, www.expedia.com, www.opodo.es, or www.travelocity.com) or by checking with the major carriers.

- **Alitalia** Ⓣ 06 2222, Ⓦ www.alitalia.com
- **American Airlines** Ⓣ 06 6605 3169, Ⓦ www.americanairlines.com/it
- **Continental Airlines** Ⓣ 06 6605 3030, Ⓦ www.continental.com
- **Delta Airlines** Ⓣ 848 780 376 toll-free, Ⓦ www.delta.com
- **United Airlines** Ⓣ 02 6963 3707, Ⓦ www.united.com
- **US Airways** Ⓣ 06 420 3261, Ⓦ www.usairways.com

IMPORTANT PHONE NUMBERS AT A GLANCE

Europe-wide emergency number	112
Medical emergency	113
Police	113
Firefighters	115

18 . EMERGENCIES

Appendix

USEFUL PHRASES

Here are some of the phrases you'll need to go about your daily life in Rome, as you study, shop, get together with friends, and make your way around the city.

NUMBERS

Phrase	Translation	Pronunciation
0	zero	TZE-ro
1	uno	OO-no
2	due	DOO-e
3	tre	tre
4	quattro	KWA-tro
5	cinque	CHEEN-kwe
6	sei	se
7	sette	SE-te
8	otto	O-to
9	nuove	NO-ve
10	dieci	dee-E-chee
11	undici	OON-dee-chee
12	dodici	DO-dee-chee
13	tredici	TRE-dee-chee
14	quattordici	kwa-TOR-dee-chee
15	quindici	KWEEN-dee-chee
16	sedici	SE-dee-chee
17	diciassette	dee-cha-SE-te
18	diciotto	dee-CHO-to
19	diciannove	dee-cha-NO-ve
20	venti	VEN-tee
21	ventuno	ven-TOO-no
22	ventidue	ven-tee-DOO-e
30	trenta	TREN-ta
40	quaranta	kwa-RAN-ta
50	cinquanta	cheen-KWAN-ta
60	sessanta	se-SAN-ta
70	settanta	se-TAN-ta
80	ottanta	o-TAN-ta
90	novanta	no-VAN-ta
100	cento	CHEN-to
200	duecento	DOO-e-chen-to

500	cinquecento	CHEEN-kwe-chen-to
1,000	mille	MEE-le
100,000	centomila	chen-to-MEE-la
1,000,000	un milione	oon mee-LYO-ne
first	primo/a	PREE-mo
second	secondo/a	se-CON-do
third	terzo/a	TER-tzo
fourth	quarto/a	KWAR-to
fifth	quinto/a	KWEEN-to
sixth	sesto/a	SES-to
seventh	settimo/a	SE-tee-mo
eighth	ottavo/a	o-TAV-o
ninth	nono/a	NO-no
tenth	decimo/a	DE-chee-mo
one-half/ a half	mezzo/a	ME-tzo
one-third/ a third	un terzo	oon TER-tzo
one-fourth/ a quarter	un quarto	oon KWAR-to

DAYS OF THE WEEK

Monday	lunedì	loo-ne-DEE
Tuesday	martedì	mar-te-DEE
Wednesday	mercoledì	mer-co-le-DEE
Thursday	giovedì	jo-ve-DEE
Friday	venerdì	ve-ner-DEE
Saturday	sabato	SA-ba-to
Sunday	domenica	do-ME-nee-ka

MONTHS

January	gennaio	je-NAI-o
February	febbraio	fe-BRAI-o
March	marzo	MAR-tzo
April	aprile	a-PREE-le
May	maggio	MA-jo
June	giugno	JOO-nyo
July	luglio	LOO-lyo
August	agosto	a-GO-sto
September	settembre	se-TEM-bre
October	ottobre	o-TO-bre

November	novembre	no-VEM-bre
December	dicembre	di-CHEM-bre

EMERGENCIES & GETTING HELP

Help!
Aiuto!
ay-OO-to!

Can you help me?
Puoi aiutarmi?
pwoy ay-oo-TAR-mee?

Hurry!
Presto!
PRES-to!

Call an ambulance!
Chiama un'ambulanza!
KYA-ma oo-nam-boo-LAN-za!

Someone is hurt.
Qualcuno è danneggiato.
kwal-COO-no eh dan-eh-JA-to.

I need the fire department.
Ho bisogno del reparto di fuoco.
o bee-ZO-nyo del re-PAR-to d FWO-ko.

I smell smoke.
Sento l'odore del fumo.
SEN-to lo-dor-e del FU-mo.

There's a fire in my apartment/apartment building.
Ci è un fuoco nella mia appartamento/nel mio edificio
appartamento.
Chee ay oon FWO-ko nella MEE-uh a-part-a-MENT-o.

Call the police!
Chiama la polizia!
KYA-ma la pol-ee-TZEE-a!

I need to report a crime.
Devo segnalare un crimine.
DAY-vo sen-ya-LA-re oon CREE-mee-ne.

I was assaulted.
Mi hanno aggredito.
mee A-no a-gre-DEE-to.

I was mugged.
Mi hanno rapinato.
me A-no ra-pee-NA-to.

I lost . . .
Ho perso . . .
o PER-so . . .

Someone stole . . .
Mi hanno rubato . . .
mee A-no roo-BA-to . . .

My wallet/purse/passport/cell phone
il portafoglio/la borsa/il passaporto/il cellulare
eel por-ta-FO-lyo/la BOR-sa/eel pa-sa-POR-to | eel che-loo-LA-re

My address is . . .
Il mio indirizzo è . . .
il MEE-o in-dee-REE-zo eh...

My number is . . .
Il mio numero è . . .
eel MEE-o NOO-ma-ro eh . . .

I am on the ___ floor.
Sono in ___ piano.
SO-no in ___ pee-AN-o.

GREETINGS & INTRODUCTIONS

Hello!
Ciao!
chow!

Good morning/afternoon/evening!
Buongiorno/buon pomeriggio/buonasera
bwon-JOR-no|bwon po-me-REE-jo|bwo-na-SE-ra!

How are you?
Come stai?
ko-me stai?

I'm great/not so great.
Sto benissimo/non benissimo.
sto ben-EE-see-mo|non ben-EE-see-mo.

What's up?
Che mi racconti?
ke me era-KON-tee?

Nothing much.
Niente di speciale.
NYEN-te dee spe-CHA-le.

What's your name?
Come ti chiami?
ko-me tee KYA-mee?

My name is . . .
Mi chiamo . . .
mee KYA-mo . . .

Pleased to meet you.
Piacere (di conoscerti).
pya-CHE-re (dee co-no-SHER-tee).

Where are you from?
Di dove sei?
dee DO-ve SE-i?

APPENDIX: USEFUL PHRASES

Are you from here?
Sei di qua?
se dee kwa?

I'm from the United States.
Sono di Stati Uniti.
SO-no dee STA-tee oo-NEE-tee.

I'm a student at . . .
Sono un studente (una studentessa) a . . .
SO-no OO-na stew-den-TESS-a a . . .

I study . . .
Studio . . .
STEW-deeo . . .

Where do you live?
Dove abiti?
DO-vay AH-bee-tee?

I live . . .
Abito a . . .
AH-bee-to ah . . .

Is this seat/table taken?
Questa sede/tavola è occupata?
KWES-ta SE-de oku-PA-ta?

How long will you be in Rome?
Quanto tempo stai a Roma?
KWAN-to TEM-po sti a RO-ma?

This is my friend . . .
Ciò è il mio amico . . .
CHO eh il MEE-o a-MEE-co . . .

Goodbye.
Arrivederci.
a-ree-ve-DER-chee.

See you later/tomorrow.
A più tardi/a domattina.
a pyoo TAR-dee/a do-ma-TEE-na.

GETTING CONNECTED

What's your email?
Qual'è la tua email?
kwal eh la too-a ee-MEIL?

What's your phone number?
Che cosa è il tuo numero di telefono?
ke CO-za eh il NOO-me-ro d tel-E-fono?

I'll call you.
Ti telefonerò.
tee te-le-fon-e-RO.

Call me sometime.
Mi telefoni.
me te-LEH-fo-ni.

What's your address?
Che cosa è il tuo indirizzo?
ke CO-za eh il TOO-o in-di-RI-zo?

PLEASANTRIES

Please.
Per favore.
per fa-VO-re.

Thank you.
Grazie.
GRA-tzee-e.

You're welcome.
Prego.
PRE-go.

Excuse me.
Scusami.
SKOO-za-mee.

Sorry.
Scusa.
SKOO-za.

ON CAMPUS

Where/When is your next class?
Dove/quando è la tua seguente classe?
DO-ve/KWAN-do e la too-a se-GUEN-te CLA-say?

Did you study?
Hai studiato?
ai stu-di-AH-to?

Can I look at your notes?
Posso guardare le tue note?
PO-so gwar-DA-re lay too-e NO-te?

Want to meet after class?
Hai voglio di contatto di dopo la classe?
ai VO-leeo di con-TA-to do DO-po la CLA-say?

I'm going to the library.
Vado in biblioteca.
VA-do in bib-li-o-TEC-a.

Can I borrow your textbook?
Posso prendere in prestito il tuo manuale?
PO-so PREN-de-re in pres-TI-to il TOO-o man-oo-AHLAY?

I forgot my homework.
Ho dimenticato i compiti.
o dee-men-ti-CA-to ee COM-pee-tee.

I need an extension.
Ho bisogno di un'estensione
o bee-ZON-nyo di oon es-ten-SION-ne.

What grade did you get?
Che grado hai ottenuto?
ke GRA-do ai o-ten-OO-to?

Do you have any idea what's going on?
Sai che cosa sta accendendo?
sai ke CO-za sta a-chen-DEN-do?

I need coffee.
Ho bisogno di un caffe.
o be-ZONEEO d OON ca-FAY.

LANGUAGE

Do you speak English?
Parli inglese?
PAR-lee een-GLE-ze?

I speak English.
Parlo inglese.
PAR-lo een-GLE-ze.

I don't speak Italian.
Non parlo italiano.
non PAR-lo ee-tal-YAN-o.

I speak only a little Italian.
Parlo solo un po' d'italiano.
PAR-lo SO-lo oon po dee-tal-YA-no.

I don't understand.
Non capisco.
non kap-EE-sko.

Do you understand me?
Mi hai capito?
mee ai ca-PEE-to?

Speak more slowly, please.
Parli più lentamente, per favore.
PAR-lee pyoo len-ta-MEN-te, per fa-VO-re.

Can you repeat that, please?
Ripeta, per favore?
ree-PET-ah, per fa-VO-re?

DIRECTIONS & GETTING AROUND

Where is . . .
Dov'è . . .
do-VE . . .

What is the address?
Che cosa è l'indirizzo?
ke CO-za E lin-di-REE-zio?

Left
a sinistra
a see-NEE-stra

Right
a destra
a DE-stra

Across from
attraverso da
ah-tra-VAIR-so da

Next to
vicino a
vee-CHEE-no ah

Behind
dietro
dee-AY-tro

In front of
davanti
da-VAHN-tee

Where's the nearest metro/bus stop?
Dov'è la fermata della metro/dell'autobus più vicina?
do-VE la fer-MA-ta de-la ME-tro/de-lau-to-BOOS pyoo vee-CHEE-na?

Where can I catch a taxi?
Dove posso prendere un taxi?
DO-ve PO-so PREN-de-re oon TA-ksee?

SHOPPING

Open
aperto
a-PER-to

Closed
chiuso
ki-OO-zo

Can I try it on?
Posso provarlo/la?
PO-so pro-VAR-lo?

How much does this cost?
Quanto costa questo?
KWAN-to ko-sta KWE-sto?

I'm just browsing.
Sto solo guardando.
sto SO-lo gwar-DAN-do.

Do you sell . . .
Vendete . . .
ven-DE-te . . .

It doesn't fit me.
Non mi sta.
non mee sta.

Do you have something in a larger/smaller size?
Ha qualcosa in una taglia più grande/piccola?
a kwal-KO-za een oo-na TA-lya pyoo GRAN-de/PEE-ko-la?

Do you take credit cards?
Prendete carte di credito?
pren-DE-te KAR-ta dee KRE-dee-to?

I'd like to buy this.
Vorrei comprare questo.
vo-RAY com-PRAH-re KWES-to.

Is this returnable?
Posso ritornare questo?
PO-so ree-tor-NA-re KWES-to?

EATING OUT

Where should we eat?
Dove dobbiamo mangiare?
DO-vay do-bi-A-mo man-JA-re?

Is it cheap?
È conveniente?
eh kon-ven-YEN-te?

Is it nearby?
È vicino?
eh vee-CHEE-no?

What kind of food do they serve?
Che tipo di cibo fanno?
ke TEE-po dee CHEE-bo FA-no?

Can they take a big group?
Prendono gruppi?
PREN-do-no GROO-pee?

How late do they serve food?
Fino a che ora danno da mangiare?
FEE-no a ke O-ra DA-no da man-JA-re?

We'd like a table for four.
Vorremmo un tavolo per quattro.
vo-RE-mo oon TA-vo-lo per KWA-tro.

I'm waiting for someone.
Aspetto per qualcuno.
ah-SPE-to per kwal-COO-no.

My friends will be here soon.
I miei amici saranno qui presto.
ee myay a-MEE-chee sa-RA-no kwee PRE-sto.

May I see a menu?
Posso vedere il menu?
PO-so VE-de-re eel me-NOO?

I'll have . . .
Vorrei . . .
vo-RE . . .

The check, please.
Il conto, per favore.
eel KON-to, per fa-VO-re.

GOING OUT

What are you up to tonight?
Che hai voglia di fare stasera?
ke ai VO-lya dee FA-re sta-SE-ra?

You feel like doing something?
Hai voglia di fare qualcosa?
ai VO-lya dee FA-re kwal-KO-za?

What do you feel like doing?
Che ti va di fare?
ke tee va dee FA-re?

I'm in the mood to . . .
Ho voglia di . . .
o VO-lya dee . . .

What time do you want to meet?
A che ora vuoi che ci vediamo?
a ke O-ra vwoy ke chee ve-DYA-mo?

I'm running late.
Sono in ritardo.
SO-no een ree-TAR-do.

I'm ready!
Sono pronto/a!
SO-no PRON-to!

Where do you want to meet?
Dove vuoi che ci vediamo?
DO-ve vwoy ke chee ve-DYA-mo?

I'll meet you there.
Ci vediamo là.
chee ve-DYA-mo la.

Do you have money?
Hai dei soldi?
ai de-ee SOL-dee?

Are you bringing a bag?
Ti porti la borsa?
tee POR-tee la BOR-sa?

What are you going to wear?
Cosa ti metti?
KO-za tee ME-tee?

APPENDIX: USEFUL PHRASES

Is there dancing?
Si balla?
see BA-la?

Let's go somewhere else.
Andiamo da qualche altra parte.
an-DYA-mo da KWAL-ke AL-tra PAR-te.

Is there an ATM around here?
C'è un bancomat qua vicino?
che oon BAN-ko-mat kwa vee-CHEE-no?

CONVERSIONS

U.S. TO METRIC

1 in	25.4 mm
1 in	2.54 cm
1 ft	0.3 m
1 sq. ft	0.09 sq. m
1 mile	1.6 km
1 lb	0.45 kg
1 lb	0.07 stone (U.K.)
1 oz	28 g
1 gallon	3.79 liters

METRIC TO U.S.

1 mm	0.039 in
1 cm	0.39 in
1 m	3.28 ft
1 sq. m	10.76 sq. ft
1 km	0.62 mile
1 kg	2.2 lb
1 stone (U.K.)	14 lb
1 g	0.04 oz
1 liter	0.26 gallons

TEMPERATURE

$C = F - 32 / 1.8$
$F = C \times 1.8 + 32$

CLOTHING SIZES

Important note: These sizes are approximate. Always try things on before you buy them. Also note that in the United Kingdom, shoes are not always sold in half sizes, and some stores sell shoes in European or U.S. sizes.

WOMEN'S CLOTHES

U.S.	4	6	8	10	12	14
U.K.	6	8	10	12	14	16
Europe	34	36	38	40	42	44

MEN'S CLOTHES

U.S./U.K.	35	36	37	38	39	40
Europe	46	48	50	52	54	56

WOMEN'S SHOES

U.S.	5	6	7	8	9	10
U.K.	3.5	4.5	5.5	6.5	7.5	8.5
Europe	36	37	39	40	41	42

MEN'S SHOES

U.S.	7	8	9	10	11	12
U.K.	6.5	7.5	8.5	9.5	10.5	11.5
Europe	40	41	42	44	45	47

COUNTRY CODES

Here are some commonly used country codes in Western Europe and North America. Note that many European phone numbers start with a 0, which should only be used when dialing within the country.

Austria	43
Belgium	32
Canada	1
Denmark	45
Finland	358
France	33
Germany	49
Greece	30
Italy	39
Netherlands	31
Norway	47
Poland	48
Portugal	351
Republic of Ireland	353
Spain	34
Sweden	46
Switzerland	41
United Kingdom	44
United States	1

ABOUT THE WRITER

Kim Westerman first visited Italy in 1991, and it became her adopted home after she learned how to say "Brunello." She now lives in Berkeley, CA, and is the managing editor of *Wine Business Monthly*. She launched a travel website, throughtraveler.com, in 2003 and writes frequently about food, wine spas, and travel. Her work has appeared in *The New York Times,* Fodor's travel guides, Moon Metro guides, *Epicurious, CondeNet, TASTE Magazine,* and Expedia's *Home & Abroad.*

PHOTO CREDITS

1. **Paperwork & Practicalities** © Karen Barr Sutorius
2. **The Neighborhoods** © Karen Barr Sutorius
3. **Getting Around** © Danilo Ascione/Shutterstock
4. **Finding Housing** © PhotoDisc Vol 22/iStockphoto
5. **Shopping** © Kerry Muzzey/Shutterstock
6. **Daily Living** © Clara Natoli/Shutterstock
7. **Studying & Staying Informed** © Vixique/Shutterstock
8. **Staying in Touch** © Ron Chapple/ThinkStock/iStockphoto
9. **Health** © Anthony Hall/iStockphoto
10. **Getting Involved** © Andrea Seemann/Shutterstock
11. **Working** © Andreas Guskos/iStockphoto
12. **Fitness & Beauty** © Luke Daniek/iStockphoto
13. **Sports** © Elena Sherengovskaya/Shutterstock
14. **Cultural Activities** © Kevin Jordan/Corbis
15. **Eating Out** © Gianluca Figliola Fantini/Shutterstock
16. **Night Life** © Emmanelle Morand/ Paulette/Fotolia
17. **Going Away** © Maria Valentino/iStockphoto
18. **Emergencies** © Pierrette Guertin/iStockphoto

INDEX

A

Abbacchio a scottadito (lamb chops), 161
Abbey Theatre Pub, 29, 107
Abortion, 105–106
Absentee voting, 15
Academic year, 4
Accademia del Nuoto (swimming pool), 129
Accademia Tedesca a Villa Massimo, 148
Adaptors, 76
Advil, 125
Agenzia Intermediate (au pair agency), 124
Aggressive drivers, 188
Agnolotti (stuffed pastas), 161
AIM, 94
Air Berlin, 183
Air Europa, 183
Air One, 183
Air travel:
    baggage restrictions, 184
    cheap flights, 189
    restrictions and limitations, 184
    surcharges, 184
Airports:
    secondary, 184
    taxis/city buses/shuttle buses to, 42
Akab Cave (club), 114, 172, 175
Alcazar (theater), 27
Alessandrina Library at La Sapienza University, 80
Alexanderplatz (jazz club), 173
Alien (club), 172, 175
Alitalia (airline), 199
Almost Corner Bookshop, 82
Alpheus (club), 173, 175
Amaro (after-dinner drink), 177
Ambrit International School, 122
Ambulance, 193
American Airlines, 199
American Automobile Association (AAA), 186

American Express, 69
American Hospital, 104
American movies, 29
American Overseas School of Rome, 122
American products, 16
American-style breakfast, 95
Amrita Centro Yoga e Ayurveda (yoga/Pilates), 131
Angels Staff Services Association (au pair agency), 124
Anglo American Bookstore, 82
Anima (bar), 171, 175
Annibale (butcher), 60
Anti-Americanism, v
Antico Arco (restaurant), 162
Antipasto (appetizer), 158
Apartments, 73–77
    brokers, 48–49
    cable/television, 73–74
    dryers, 53
    electricity, 74
    elevators, 53
    garbage, 75
    gas, 74
    gas stoves, 53
    Internet, 74
    leasing, 50–51
    listings, 46–48
    locksmiths, 75
    maintenance, 75
    microwaves, 53
    prices, 49–50
    quirks, 53
    recycling, 75–76
    sharing, 46
    space, 53
    telephones, 74–75
    utilities, 73–74
Appian Way, 77
Arancia Blu (vegetarian restaurant), 163
Arcigay (LGBT organization), 116
Arrests, 195–196
Art, 189
AS Roma football jersey, 65

Asinocotto (restaurant), 162
assioma.org, 120
Assisi (medieval town), 189
Associazione per l'Educazione
    Demografica (AIED), 106
ATAC, 33
        lost and found, on buses, 197
ATMs, 68–70
Au pair work, 123–124
        pay, 124
Auditorium (for classical music),
    149
Aula Magna dell'Universita in
    Sapienza (for classical music),
    149
Aula Ottagona, 189
Auto Europe, 187
Aveda Day Spa, 132
Aventine Hill, 26
Avis Car Rental, 187
Avventure Bellissime (tours), 146

B

Baby Bear Household Services (au
    pair work), 124
Baggage restrictions, 184
Bakeries (*panetteries/pasticceries*),
    58–59
Ballet/dance, 147–148
Banca Intesa, 72
Banca Nazionale del Lavoro, 72
Banco di Siclia, 72
Bar del Fico, 165, 171
Bar gli Archi, 29
Barbershops, 131–132
Bars, 111, 170–171
Basilica di San Clemente, 21
Basilica di Santa Maria in
    Trastevere, 27
Basilica di Santa Maria Maggiore, 20
Beauty products, 125, *See also*
    Fitness/beauty
Befana (Epiphany), 153
Bella Vita Italia (package trips/
    tours), 185
Bergamo (town), 189
Biao e Te (vegetarian restaurant),
    164
Bibli Café, 81

Biblioteca di Storia Moderna e
    Contemporanea (Library of
    Modern and Contemporary
    History), 81
Big Mama (club), 173
Biglietto Flexi, 182
Bikes, 38–39
        purchasing, 38
        renting, 38–39
        rules of the road, 39
Birth-control pills, 105
Biscotti, 58–59
Blending, 195
Bluecheese Factory (club), 174
Bmibaby airline, 183
Books, 7, 81–82
        English-language, 125
Bowling, 175
Bread bakeries (*panetterie*), 58–59
Breaks, v
Brokers, apartments, 48–49
Bruno e Massimo Necci (salon),
    131
La Buca di Bacco (gay/lesbian bar
    and lounge), 175
Bucatini (spaghetti), 161
Budget Car Rental, 187
Buongusto Tours, 185
Buses, 35–36
        to the airport, 42
        boarding, 36
        bus notturno (night bus), 35
        buying tickets, 36
        hours of operation, 35
        navigating the system, 36
        safety on, 36
Bush (club), 172
Butchers (*macellerie*), 60

C

Cable/television, 73–74
Caffé Latino, 114, 174
Calcio (soccer), 87, 136, 139, 140
Calling cards, 93
Calling home, 92–95
        direct calls, 93
        international numbers,
            dialing, 94
        Italian calling cards, 93

pay phones, 93
Voice over Internet Protocol (VoIP), 94–95
Calvary Hospital (Blue Nuns), 104
cambiolavoro.com, 120
Cambridge Certificate in English Language Teaching to Adults, 123
Camping, 139
Campo de' Fiori, 21–22, 29, 91
farmers' market, 61
spice sellers, 65
Canale 5 (channel), 85
Capitoline Hill, 117
Capitoline Museums, 21, 133, 144–145, 189
Capuchin cemetery, 133
Car rentals, 186–188
Carabinieri (police), 194–195
Card playing, 167
Cars, 39–40
rules of the road, 40
Caruso Café de Oriente, 173
Casa di Cura Assunzione di Maria, 104
Cash, 68–70
getting from home, 68–69
Cash advance, 69
Castel Sant'Angelo, 28, 133, 167
Castelli Romani Harvest Festival, 153
Castroni (grocery store), 107
Cavalieri Hilton, spa at, 132
Cell phones, 91–92
and cars/scooters, 40
contract, signing, 91–92
rechargeable SIM cards (*ricaricards*), 91
U.S. cell phone, using, 92
Cemeteries, 133
Centro Linguistico Italiano Dante Alighieri (language classes), 152
Centro Mediterraneo (language classes), 152
Centro Sportivo Cassia Nuoto (swimming pool), 129
Centro Yoga Vedanta Sivananda (yoga/Pilates), 131
charta.it, 147

Checchino dal1887 (eatery), 160
Cheese shops (*negozi del formaggio*), 59
Chiesa di San Luigi dei Francesi, 23
Chiesa di Santa Maria della Concezione, 24
Capuchin cemetery, 133
Chiesa di Santa Maria della Pace, 117
Chiesa di Santa Maria della Vittoria, 25
Chieso di Sant'ivo alla Sapienza, 23
Chiostro del Bramante, 117
Ciampino (CIA) airport, 41–42, 184
Cimitero Acattolico per gli Stranieri (cemetery), 26
Circolo Mario Mieli di Omosessuale Cultura (LGBT organization), 116
Circus Maximus (jogging site), 130
Citations, 195–196
Classical music, 149
Clothing, 16
Clothing sizes, 216
clubclassic.net, 175
Clubs, 172–173
Coda fiscale (or tax ID number), 124
Coffee-flavored liqueur, 177
COIN (one-stop shopping), 63
Cold medicines, 125
Colosseum, 2, 20–21, 117, 133, 195
Comedy, 176
Coming Out (gay pub), 175
Communication, 90–95
calling home, 92–95
cell phones, 91–92
Internet, 90
CONAD (one-stop shopping), 63
Concerts, free, 167
Condor airlines, 183
Context Travel, 185
Continental Airlines, 199
Contorno (side dish), 158
Conversions, 215
Converters, 76

Coop (supermarket chain), 56–57
Cornettificio Sorchetta Doppio
　Schizzo (all-night pastry shop),
　165
Corno (pl. cornetti), 3, 59, 87
Corriere della Sera (newspaper),
　83, 120
COTRAL (lost and found, in
　metro), 197
Country codes, 94, 217
Craigslist Rome (rome.craigslist.
　org), 111, 120
Credit cards, 16, 70
　lost/stolen, canceling, 197
Cul de Sac (cafe), 160
Cultural activities, 143–155
　festivals/holidays, 152–154
　films, 150–152
　galleries, 144–145
　guided sightseeing tours, 146
　museums, 144–145
　performing arts, 147–150
Culture, 3
　immersing yourself in, v
Culture shock, v
Customer service, 95
Cycling, 136, 137–138
　rules of the road, 39

D

Da Baffetto (pizzeria), 159, 164
Da Gigetto (Roman-Jewish
　cuisine), 160
Da Paris (Roman-Jewish cuisine),
　160
Daily living, 67–77
　adaptors, 76
　American Express, 69
　apartments, 73–77,
　ATMs, 68–70
　cash, 68–70
　cash advance, 69
　converters, 76
　credit cards, 70
　dry cleaning, 76
　exchanging money, 70, 69–70
　international money transfers,
　　69
　Italian bank accounts, 71–72
　laundry, 76
　postal services, 72–73
　U.S. checks, cashing, 69
　Western Union, 69
　wiring money, 69
Dar Poeta (pizzeria), 159
Date spots, 162–163
Dating, 111–112
Day trips, 155
Days of the week, 203
Dei Gracchi, 22
Delta Airlines, 199
Dentists, 103
Designer jeans, 95
DF Serrature Porte, 75
DHL, 73
Dinner:
　with family, 159–160
　with friends, 158
Direct calls, 93
Directions, phrases for, 210–211
Disabled travelers, 42
Discussion group, joining, 111
Ditirambo (restaurant), 160–161
Doctor visits, 103–104
Dog waste, 43
La Dolce Vita Tours, 185
Dolci (dessert), 158
Dome Rock Café, 174
Drinking legally, 174
Drinks, 177
Drunken Ship, The (bar), 171
Dry cleaning, 76

E

EasyCar, 187
EasyInternet Café, 90
EasyJet, 42, 183
easyjob.it, 120
Eating out, 5
Eco Move Rent, 39
Economist, The (magazine), 84–85
Ecstasy of Santa Teresa (sculpture),
　25
Electricity, 74
Emergencies:
　citations/arrests, 195–196
　important phone numbers,
　　192–195

lost/stolen property, 196–197
   passport, 197–198
   phrases for, 204–205
   safety basics, 195
   unexpected trips home,
      198–199
Emergency rooms, 104
Emperors of Rome, The (theater
   troupe), 148–149
ENEL (Ente Nazionale per
   l'Energia Elettrica), 74
English Bookshop, The, 82
English-language books/
   magazines, 125
English-language bookstores,
   82–83
English-language movies, 95
English-language newspapers, 84
English-speaking hospitals,
   obtaining list of, 104
English Yellow Pages, 84, 113, 120,
   123
Enjoy Rome (tours), 146
Erasmus, 114
Esposizione Universale di Roma
   (EUR), 2, 77, 141
Esquiline, 20–21
Eurail Pass:
Eurail National Pass, 181
Eurail Select Pass and Eurail
   Regional Pass, 181
Eurailpass Global Pass Flexi, 181
   website, 180
Eurolines (bus service), 182
Euromobilia Centro Europeo del
   Mobile (home furnishings), 63
Europcar, 187
Europe-wide emergency services
   number (112), 192–193, 199
Eurosat (satellite service), 73
Eurostar (ES) trains, 182
Eurostar (trains), 41
Evening *passeggiatas* (strolls), 87
Exchange rate, 120
Exchanging money:
   at airports, 70
   at banks, 70
   at exchange counters, 70
   exchange rates, 69–70

Expat Exchange, 113, 120
Expat resources, 113–114
Expats in Italy, 114
Expedia (travel website), 188, 199

F

Fabrizio (salon), 131
Family visas, 13–14
Farmacia Fabiana, 101
Farmacia Internaazionale
   Apotheke, 101
Farmacia Trinita dei Monti, 101
Farmers' markets, 5, 60–62
Farnese Fitness (gym), 129
Federal Express, 73
Feltrinelli International, 83
Ferragosto (Assumption), 153
Festa di Noantri (Feast of We
   Others), 153
Festivals/holidays, 152–154
Fiddler's Elbow (bar), 171
Film festivals, 151
Films, 7, 150–152
   film festivals, 151
   movie theaters, 152–153
Filo Diretto, 100
Fire (emergency number 115),
   194, 199
First dates, 112
Fishmongers, 60
Fitness/beauty, 127–133
   gyms and sports clubs,
      128–129
   hair salons and barbershops,
      131–132
   high-end salons/beauty shops,
      128
   running routes, 130
   spas, 132
   swimming pools, 129
   yoga/Pilates, 130–131
Fitness Express DIFOSTER, 129
Flea markets, 62
Fleming Fitness, 129
Florence, 155
flylc.com, 183
Fontina (cheese), 59
Food/eating/cooking, 157–167
   date spots, 162–163

dinner with family, 159–160
dinner with friends, 158
late-night food, 164–165
lunch/food to go, 165–166
phrases for, 212–213
pizza, 164
Roman cuisine, 161
tipping in restaurants, 160
vegan/vegetarian foods,
  163–164
Food shopping, 5
Forms DS-11 and DS-64, 198
Frangelico (after-dinner drink),
  177
Free attractions, 189
Free concerts, 167
Free events, 6
Friendships, 112
Fritto misto (mixed fry), 161
FS (lost and found in trains), 197

G

Galleria Borghese, 133
Galleria Nazionale d'Arte, 145
Galleria Nazionale d'Arte
  Moderna, 145
Garage Sale, Rigattiere per hobby,
  62
Garbage, 75
Gas, 74
Gas leaks (emergency number 800
  803 020), 194
Gas stations, 40
Gay/lesbian community:
  bars and clubs, 175
  LGBT organizations, 116
  gaymap.info/rome, 175
  gayrome.com, 175
  gaytour.it, 175
Il Gelatone (vegetarian restaurant),
  164
Gente Viaggi (magazine), 85
Germanwings airline, 183
Giardino do Sisto V (outdoor
  performances), 147–148
Gifts, 65
Il Giornale, 83
Global Experiences, 121
Global medical insurance, 100

Gnocchi, 161
Google Talk, 94
Gorgonzola (cheese), 59
Grana Padano (cheese), 59
Grappa (drink), 177
Grappolo d'Oro (eatery), 165
Green Line Tours, 146
Greenpeace, 115
Greetings/introductions, phrases
  for, 206–207
Grocery shopping, 56–58
  hours of operation, 56
  lexicon, 58
  milk, 57
  produce, 57
  quantities, 57
Gruppi Archeologici d'Italia
  (Archaeological Groups of Italy),
  115
Guided sightseeing tours, 146
Gusto (eatery), 107, 161
Gyms, 128–129
Gynecologists, 104

H

Hair salons, 131–132
Halal food stalls, 62
L'Hangar (gay club), 175
Hapag Lloyd Express, 183
Happy Cow, 62, 163
Headache medicines, 125
Health, 97–107
  abortion, 105–106
  dentists, 103
  doctor visits, 103–104
  emergency rooms, 104
  gynecologists, 104
  hospitals, 104
  Italian healthcare system,
    99–100
  mental-health professionals,
    104
  optometrists/
    ophthalmologists, 103–104
  pharmacies, 101–102
  physicians, 103
  sexual health issues, 105–106
  sexual health organizations,
    106

Health insurance, 15–16, 98–100
Hello Ticket, 150
Helplines, 105
Hertz, 187
High-end knock-offs, 65
High-traffic shopping areas, 64
Hiking, 136, 136–137
Hills of Rome, 117
Historic jogging tours, 130
Holiday Autos, 187
Home furnishings, 63–64
Homesickness, conquering, 107
Homestays, 51–52
Horseback riding, 139
Hospitals, 104
Hotel de Russie, spa at, 132
Housing, 15, 45–53
    apartments, 48–49, 50–51,
      53, 46
    homestays, 51–52
Hunger, 87

I

Ikea (home furnishings), 63
Illegal alien status, 14
Important phone numbers,
    192–195
    Europe-wide emergency
      services number (112),
      192–193, 199
    fire (emergency number 115),
      194, 199
    gas leaks (emergency number
      800 803 020), 194
    medical emergencies, 193, 199
    police (emergency number
      113), 194–195, 199
Informer, The (online publication),
    84
Institute for the International
    Education of Students, 121
insuremytrip.com, 101
InterCity (IC) trains, 41, 182
Intern Abroad, 121
International Herald Tribune, 84
International Internships, 121
International money transfers, 69
International numbers, dialing, 94

International Student Exchange
    Card (ISE Card), 5
International Student Identity
    Card (ISIC), 5, 15
International students, meeting,
    114–115
internazionalibnlditalia.it, 140
Internet, 74, 90
Internships, 121
Intramural sports team, joining, 111
Invitations, 112
Involtini (rolled strips of meat,
    stuffed), 161
Isola del Cinema (movie theater),
    151
Istituto Dante Alighieri (language
    classes), 131
Istituto Nazionale delle
    Assicurazioni, 100
ITALGAS (gas service), 74
Italia Uno (television channel), 85
Italian bank accounts, 71–72
    account checklist, 72
    banking hours, 71
    opening an account, 71–72
Italian coffee, 65
Italian drivers, caution about, 188
Italian drugstores, 101–102
Italian healthcare system, 99–100
    eligibility for, 99
    getting health coverage under,
      100
Italian Labor Ministry, 124
Italian Open, 140
Italian universities, teaching
    English at, 122

J

Janiculum Hill, 26, 117, 165, 167
Jaywalking, 95
Jazz Café, 174
Jeans, 95
Jewish Ghetto, 21–22, 62
Job hunting, 120–121
jobpilot.it, 120
Jobs, types, 121–124
Jogging tours, 130
Journal, v

K

Karaoke, 176
Kosher foods:
    butchers/restaurants, 62
    pizza, 166

L

Landline rates, 74, 93
Language, practicing, v
Language classes, 152
Language exchanges, 111
Language schools, teaching
    English at, 122
Largo 16 Ottobre, 22
Late-night food, 164–165
Laundry, 76
Laurea breve (three-year degree
    program), 4
Laurea normale (five-year degree
    program), 4
Lavanderie (laundromats), 76
Lawyer, calling, 196
Lazzaretti (bikes), 38–39
Le Sette (television station), 85
Leasing an apartment, 50–51
Leonardo da Vinci Fiumicino
    Airport (FCO), 41–42
L'espresso (magazine), 85
Levis, 95
LGBT organizations, 116
Libraries, 81–82
Light of Rome, 117
Limoncello (lemon liquer), 177
Line cutting, 43
Lion Bookshop, 83
Listings, apartments, 46–48
Live music, 173–174
Il Locale, 174
Locals:
    dining like, 117
    meeting, v
Locksmiths, 75
Long-distance calls, 74
Lost-and-found offices, 196–197
Lost/stolen credit cards, canceling,
    197
Lost/stolen property, 196–197
Lunch/food to go, 165–166

Luxuries to request from home,
    125

M

Magazines, 84–85
    English-language, 125
Maggiore, 187
Mailboxes, Etc., 73
Maintenance, 75
maratonadiroma.it, 140
Il Margutta vegetariano
    (vegetarian restaurant), 164
Mario Mieli Cultural Association,
    105
Mascarpone (cheese), 59
Massenzio (movie theater), 151
Mausoleo di Augusto, 189
Max (magazine), 85
McDonald's, 107
Media World, 94
Medical emergencies number
    (113), 193, 199
Meetup (website), 114
Men's clothing sizes, 216
Men's shoe sizes, 216
Mental-health professionals, 104
Metric to U.S. measurement
    conversions, 215
Metro, 32–35
    buying tickets, 34–35
    individual ride (BIT), 35
    monthly pass, 35
    navigating the system, 33–34
    one-day unlimited (big), 35
    one-week unlimited (CIS), 35
    student discounts, 35
    three-day unlimited (BTI), 35
Micca Club, 174
Midterm break, 189
Ministry of Foreign Affairs, 11
Ministry of Health website, 100
Miro (southern Italy cuisine), 159
Mobilnovo (home furnishings), 64
Months, 203–204
Morning-after pill, 105
Moves Fitness Center (yoga/
    Pilates), 131
Movies, 5
    American, 29

English-language, 95
Mozzarella (cheese), 59
Municipio ROMA XI, Ostiense, 82
Municipio ROMA XVI, Monteverde Nuevo, 82
Museo d'Arte Contemporanea (MACRO), 23
Museo della Civiltà Romana (Museum of Roman Civilization), 77
Museo di Roma, 27
Museo e Galleria Borghese, 145
Museo Nazionale Etrusco di Villa Giulia, 145
Mussolini, Benito, 2, 22
Myair Airlines, 183

N

Natale (Christmas), 154
National Epidemiological Bulletin, 106
Neighborhoods, 19–29
    Colosseum/Esquiline, 20–21
      farmers' markets, 61
    Jewish Ghetto/Campo de' Fiori, 21–22
    new, discovering, 141
    Nomentano, 22
    Piazza Navona/Pantheon, 23
    Spanish Steps/Via Vittorio/ Veneto/Parioli, 24
    Stazione Termini/San Lorenzo, 25
    Testaccio, 25–26
    Trastevere, 26–27, 29
    Vatican City, 27–28
Networking, and job hunting, 120–121
New School, The, 122
Newspapers, 83–84
    in English, 84
    and job hunting, 120
Newsweek, 84–85
Nightlife, 169–177
    bars, 170–171
    bowling, 175
    clubs, 172–173
    comedy, 176
    drinking legally, 174

gay/lesbian bars and clubs, 175
    karaoke, 176
    live music, 173–174
Nomads Adventure Card, 186
Non Solo Pizza, 165
Nonalcoholic drinks, 177
Norwegian airlines, 183
Notti di Cinema a Piazza di Vittorio (movie theater), 151
Nulla Osta (letter), 13
Numbers, 202–203
Nuovo Sacher (movie theaters), 151

O

Ombre Rosse (pub), 159
Omnitel (Internet service provider), 74
One-stop shopping, 63
Online financial statements, 15
Opera, 147
Opodo (travel company), 188, 199
Optometrists/ophthalmologists, 103–104
Orbitz (travel website), 188, 199
Organ meats, 161
Orvieto, 155
Ostia Antica, 155
Ostia Beach, 155
Ostriche a Colazione (restaurant), 162
Over-the-counter drugs, 16, 102
Oviessa (one-stop shopping), 63

P

Package trips and tours, 184–185
Palatine Hill, 21
Panettoni, 59
Pannattoni (pizzeria), 159
Pantheon, 23, 87, 117
Paperwork, getting in order, 124
Parco dei Caduti (Park of the Fallen), 25
Parmigiano Reggiano (cheese), 59
Pasquino (movie theaters), 151
Passetto di Borgo, 153
Passport, 10–11, 15
    loss of, 11
    photocopy of, 16
    replacing, 197–198

Pasta, 5
Pastry shops (*pasticcerie*), 58–59
Pay phones, 93
Peanut butter, 125
Pecorino romano (cheese), 59
Pecorino (sheep's milk cheese), 59
Performing arts, 147–150
    ballet/dance, 147–148
    classical music, 149
    opera, 147
    theater, 148–149
    tickets, 150
La Pergola (restaurant), 162
PerilloTours, 185
Permesso di soggiorno per lavoro (work card), 124
Permesso di soggiorno (visitor's permit), 12
Pharmacies, 101–102
    over-the-counter drugs, 102
    prescription drugs, 102
Phone numbers, *See* Important phone numbers
Phrases:
    on campus, 209
    days of the week, 203
    directions, 210–211
    eating out, 212–213
    emergencies, 204–205
    getting around, 210–211
    getting connected, 208
    going out, 213–215
    greetings/introductions, 206–207
    language, 210
    months, 203–204
    numbers, 202–203
    pleasantries, 208
    shopping, 211–212
Physicians, 103
Piazza Barberini, 24
Piazza dei Cavalieri di Malta, 26
Piazza del Campidoglio, 133
Piazza del Popolo, 24, 39
Piazza Mattei, 22
Piazza Navona, 23, 117
Piazza San Pietro, 28
Piazza Testaccio (open-air market), 27

Piazza Venezia, 39, 133
Piazza Vittorio Market, 61
Pickpockets, 195
Pilates, 130–131
Pilates Roma (yoga/Pilates), 131
Pincio Hill (jobbing site), 130
Piperno (eatery), 161
Pizza, 164
Places to study, 80–81
Plane ticket, 15
Playland, 175
Pleasantries, phrases for, 208
Plug adaptors, 76
Police (emergency number 113), 194–195, 199
Polizia (police), 194–195
Ponte Sisto (bridge), 26
Pope, 87
Pope paraphernalia, 65
Porta Pia, 22
Porta Portese Market (flea market), 27, 62, 77
Portico d'Ottavia, 22
Postal services, 72–73
    express delivery, 73
    hours of operation, 72
    overseas packages, 72
    regular mail (*posta prioritaria*), 72
Poste Italiane, 72–73
Pre-departure physical, 15
Preconceptions, v
Prescription drugs, 16, 102
Primo (first course), 158
Private health insurance plans, 99–100
Private tutoring, 123
Pronto Taxi, 37
Pyramid tomb of Caio Cestio, 26

Q

Questura (state police office), 12–13, 194–195
Quirinetta (movie theater), 151

R

Radio, 85–86
Radio Centro Suono (channel 101.3), 86

Radio Citta Futura (channel 97.7),
86
Radio Onda Rossa (channel 87.9),
86
Radio Radicale (channel 91.5), 86
Radio Rock (channel 106.6), 86
Radio Taxi, 37
Raidue (network), 85
Raitre (network), 85
Raiuno (network), 85
Ravenna, 189
Reading group, joining, 111
Recreational sports, 136–139
    camping, 139
    cycling, 137–138
    hiking, 136–137
    horseback riding, 139
    rock climbing, 139
    soccer, 139
Recycling, 75–76
Reef (restaurant), 161
La Repubblica, 83
Required equipment, for cyclists,
39
Rete 4 (television channel), 85
Riparte Café, 165
    bar, 171
    restaurant, 162
Ripetta (salon), 132
Ristorante la Buca di Ripet, 161
Robitussin, 125
Rock climbing, 139
Roma C'è (weekly pamphlet), 6, 84,
150, 167
Roman baths, 189
Roman drivers, caution about, 188
Roman Forum, 21
Roman Sport Center, 129
Romano Sistemi Automatizzati
(swimming pool), 129
Romans, where to meet, 110–111
Rome:
    apartments, 73–77
    autumn in, 141
    blending in, 195
    cost of living in, 4–5
    culture, 3
    daily living, 67–77
    dog waste, 43

dress/appearance in, 43
drivers, 188
emergencies, 192–199,
    204–205
family life, 3
food/eating/cooking, 157–167
grocery shopping, 56–58
history lessons in, 141
history of, 1–3
housing, 45–53
libraries, 81–82
metro, 32–35
neighborhoods, 19–29
new neighborhoods,
    discovering in, 141
nightlife, 169–177
rock climbing, 139
pickpockets, 195
safety in, 195
scenic nature of, 130
shopping, 55–65
sports, 135–141
supermarkets, 56–58
team thieves, 195
transportation, 6, 32–43
travel, 179–189
university life, 3–4
working, 119–125
Rome American Hospital, 104
Rome City Marathon, 140
Rome questura, 12
Rome Samaritans Onlus, 105
Rosati (restaurant), 165
La Rosetta (eatery), 161
Ryanair, 42, 183

S
Safety:
    basics, 195
    on buses, 36
    for cyclists, 39
    on trams, 36
Salvator Mundi International
    Hospital, 104
Sambuca (after-dinner drink), 177
San Lorenzo, 25, 114
Santa Lucia (outdoor dining), 159
Sant'Agnese, 23
Sant'Eustachio, 177

Sat Elite Sky Digital Systems
(satellite service), 73
Scatto (click), 74–75
Scooter for Rent, 38–39
Scooters, 39–40
rules of the road, 40
Scuola Leonardo da Vinci
(language classes), 152
Secondary airports, 184
Secondo (main course), 158
Seppia (cuttlefish), 60
Sera Lella (trattoria), 162
Serafino Ambrosio (yoga/Pilates),
131
Settimio all'Arancio (restaurant),
166
Sexual health:
issues, 105–106
organizations, 106
S. G. Roma (gym), 129
Shakespeare in the Park (theater
troupe), 148–149
Shaki (cafe), 166
Sharing apartments, 46
Shopping, 55–65
farmers' markets, 60–62
flea markets, 62
gifts, 65
high-traffic shopping areas, 64
home furnishings, 63–64
one-stop, 63
phrases for, 211–212
specialty foods, 58–60
supermarkets, 56–58
Shuttle buses, to the airport, 42
Il Sistina, 149
Sistine Chapel, 27
sitejogging.it, 130
Sky Europe, 183
Skype, 95
Slow Food, 115
Small towns, 189
Smoking, 163
Soccer, 87, 136, 139, 140
Il Sole 24 Ore, 83
Songs to download, 17
sos112.info, 193
Sotto le Stelle di San Lorenzo
(movie theater), 151

Spaghetti, 161
Spanish Steps, 2, 24, 167, 195
Spas, 132
Spazio Danza (ballet/dance), 148
Special diets, 62
Specialty foods, 58–60
bakeries, 58–59
butchers, 60
cheese shops, 59
fishmongers, 60
Spectator sports, 139–140
Rome City Marathon, 140
soccer, 140
tennis, 140
Speed, and cars/scooters, 40
Sperlonga, 189
Spices, 65
Sports, 135–141
recreational, 136–139
spectator, 139–140
Sports clubs, 128–129
Spring break, 189
St Peter Moto (bikes), 38–39
St Peter's Basilica, 27
St Peter's Square, 2
STA Travel, 180
Stadio Olimpic, 136, 140
La Stampa (newspaper), 83
Star, 84
Stazione Termini, 25, 41–42, 181,
187
Stereotypes, v
Stravinskij Bar (in Hotel de
Russie), 171
Student ID, 5, 147
Student visas, 11–12, 15
checklist, 12
Study-abroad checklist, 15–16
Studying, 79–87
English-language bookstores,
82–83
libraries, 81–82
magazines, 84–85
newspapers, 83–84
places to study, 80–81
television and radio, 85–86
Suonimmagine, 74
Supermarkets, 56–58
hours of operation, 56

lexicon, 58
milk, 57
produce, 57
quantities, 57
Supermercati GS, 57, 62
Supperclub (nighclub), 114, 159, 164, 173
Surcharges, air travel, 184
Swimming pools, 129
Swing (piano bar), 171

T

T-Bone Station (eatery), 107
Tabacchi (tobacco shops), 35
Tax ID number (*coda fiscale*), 124
Taxis, 32, 37
    to the airport, 42
    fares, 37
Tazza d'Oro (eatery), 166
Tea, 125
Teaching English, 122
Teaching English as a Foreign Language (TEFL), 123
Team thieves, 195
Teatro Argentina, 141, 148–149
Teatro Belli, 148–149
Teatro Colosseo, 148–149
Teatro dell'Opera di Roma, 25, 141, 147, 176
Teatro di Marcello, 22
Teatro Flaino, 176
Teatro Ghione (for classical music), 149
Teatro Nazionale, 147, 148
Teatro Olimpico, 147, 148
Teatro Sistina, 148
Teatro Valle, 141
Telecom Italia:
Internet service provider, 74
    telephone service, 74
TeleMonteCarlo (TV station), 85
Telephones, 74–75
Television, 85–86
TEFL courses, 123
Temperature, 215
Tennis, 140
tennistickets.com, 140
Terme di Caracalla (Roman baths), 147

Terme di Diocleziano, 25
Terme di Fiuggi (spa), 132
La Terrazza dell'Eden:
    bar, 166
    restaurant, 162
Testa (bar/restaurant), 163
Testaccio, 25–26
Testaccio Farmer's Market, 61, 62
Theater, 148–149
Theater of Pompeii, 21–22
Tiber Island, 22, 133
Tiber River, 165
Ticket sales, 150
Tiger Car Rental, 187
Time magazine, 84–85
Tipping:
    in bars, 172
    in restaurants, 160
Tivoli, 155
Torre di Babele (language classes), 152
Tourist visas, 14
Trains, 40–41, *See also* Trenitalia (Italian train system)
Tram Tram (eatery), 159
Trams, 35–36
    boarding, 36
    bus notturno (night bus), 35
    buying tickets, 36
    hours of operation, 35
    navigating the system, 36
    safety on, 36
Transavia Airlines, 183
Transitions Abroad, 114, 121
Transportation, 6
    adventures in, 43
    airport transportation, 41–42
    bikes, 38–39
    buses, 35–36
    cars/scooters, 39–40
    metro, 32–35
    taxis, 37
    trains, 40–41
Trastevere, 26–27, 29, 114, 170
Trastevere Market, 61
Trattoria Ugo e Maria (restaurant), 166
Travel, 179–189
    air travel, 183

buses, 182
car rentals, 186–188
discount fares, 184
Eurail Pass, 180–181
package trips and tours,
  184–185
restrictions and limitations,
  184
secondary airports, 184
surcharges, 184
Trenitalia (Italian train system),
  180, 181–182
Travel Guard International, 100
Travel insurance, 100–101
Travel Insured International, 100
Travelers with disabilities, 42
Traveling light, 16–17
Travelocity (travel website), 188,
  199
Trenitalia (Italian train system),
  41–42, 180, 181–182
  website, 155
Treno e Scooter Rent, 39
Trevi Fountain (high-traffic
  shopping area), 64
Trifonale Food and Flower Market,
  61
Il Trillo Parlante, 176
Trimani Wine Bar, 159
Trinity Certificate in Teaching
  English to Speakers of Other
  Languages, 123
Turn signals, cars/scooters, 40
Turtle fountain, 22
Tutoring, 123
Tylenol, 125

U

Underground (flea market), 62
Unexpected trips home, 198–199
Unita Sanitaria Locale (USL),
  99–100
L'Unita, 83
United Airlines, 199
University life, 3–4
Unwanted advances, 43, 112
US Airways, 199
U.S. cell phone, using, 92
U.S. checks, cashing, 69

U.S. Citizens for Peace and
  Justice, 115
U.S. Embassy:
  calling, 193
  English-speaking hospitals,
    obtaining information on, 104
  health professionals list, 103
  and lost passport, 11
  registering with, 13
  twenty-four hour number (06
    46741), 193
  website, 196
U.S. phone numbers, dialing, 94
U.S. to metric measurement
  conversions, 215
Us Weekly, 84
Utilities, 71, 73–74

V

Vatican, 2
Vatican City, 27–28
  as high-traffic shopping area,
    64
Vatican Museums, 145–146, 189
Vatican Pharmacy, 101
Vegan/vegetarian foods, 62,
  163–164
Venerdì Santo (Good Friday), 153
Veranda del'Hotel Columbus
  (restaurant), 163
Via Borgognona, as high-traffic
  shopping area, 64
Via dei Condotti, as high-traffic
  shopping area, 64
Via dei Coronari, as high-traffic
  shopping area, 64
Via dei Giubbonari, 22
Via del Babuine, high-traffic
  shopping area, 64
Via del Biscione, 21
Via del Corso, 23
  as high-traffic shopping
    area, 64
Via del Governo Vecchio, as high-
  traffic shopping area, 64
Via della Conciliazione, 2, 28
Via di Monte Testaccio, 170–171
Via Frattina, as high-traffic
  shopping area, 64

Via Margutta, 24
Via Nazionale, high-traffic shopping area, 64
Via Panisperna, 21
Via Sannio Market (flea market), 62
Via Sistina, 24
Via Vittorio Veneto, 24
Viaggi e Sapori (magazine), 85
Viale del Galoppatoio, 57
Viator (tours), 146
Villa Ada, 77
    jogging, 130
Villa Borghese, 24, 81
Villa Celimontana, 21
Villa Doria Pamphilj, 165
    jogging, 130
Villa Mirafiori (at la Sapienza University), 81
Villa Paganini, 22
Villa Pamphilj, 117
Vineria Reggio (wine bar/cafe), 115, 163, 171
VIP Backpackers Card, 186
Visa elletiva (extended stay visa), 13
Visas:
    family, 13–14
    student, 11–12
    tourist, 14
    work, 13
Visigoths, 1–2
I Vitelloni (club), 174
Vittorio Emanuele II, 2
VIVIGAS (gas service), 74
VoIP (Voice over Internet Protocol) service, 16, 94–95
volontariato.com (volunteerism portal), 115
Volpetti (grocery store/deli), 59, 166
Volunteering, 111
    opportunities, 115
Vonage, 95
Vueling Airlines, 183

W

Walking tour, 77
Walter (salon), 132

Wanted in Rome (newspaper), 84, 111
Warner Village Moderno (movie theaters), 151
Websites, and job hunting, 120
Western Union, 69
Wiring money, 69
Women's clothing sizes, 216
Women's shoe sizes, 216
Work card (*permesso di soggiorno per lavoro*), 124
Work visas, 13, 124
    and tutoring, 123
Working, 119–125
    au pair work, 123–124
    internships, 121
    job hunting, 120–121
    jobs, types of, 121–124
    under the table, 122
    teaching English, 122
    TEFL courses, 123
    tutoring, 123
World War II, 2
World Wildlife Federation (WWF), 115

Y

Yahoo, 95
YHA (Youth Hostel Association), 186
Yoga, 130–131

Z

Zi' Fenizia (restaurant), 166